Pre-Trial and Mental Health Policy in Harris County, Texas

FRONT-END REFORMS THAT PROTECT CITIZENS, CONTROL COSTS, AND ENSURE JUSTICE

Center for Effective Justice
TEXAS PUBLIC POLICY FOUNDATION
900 Congress Avenue | Suite 400
Austin, TX 78701

Including contributions from

Sen. John Whitmire
Texas State Senate

Dave LaBahn
Association of Prosecuting Attorneys

Jerry Madden
Right on Crime

Marc Levin
Right on Crime and the Texas Public
Policy Foundation

Brooke Rollins
Texas Public Policy Foundation

Adrian Garcia
Sherriff, Harris County, Texas

Matt Alsdorf
Laura and John Arnold Foundation

Tara Boh Klute
Kentucky Pre-Trial Program

Judge Ryan Patrick
Harris County, Texas

Devon Anderson
District Attorney, Harris County, Texas

Michael Dirden
Harris County Police Department

Teresa May
Harris County Community Supervision and Corrections

Clarissa Stephens
Harris County Office of Criminal Justice Coordination

Andy Keller
Meadows Mental Health Policy Institute

Judge Oscar Hale, Jr.
Webb County, Texas

Pretrial and Mental Health in Harris County, Texas: Front-end Reforms that Protect Citizens, Control Costs, and Ensure Justice is published in the United States by Right on Crime, a project of the Texas Public Policy Foundation in partnership with the American Conservative Union Foundation and the Justice Fellowship.

TEXAS PUBLIC POLICY FOUNDATION

900 Congress Avenue, Suite 400 | Austin, TX 78701

For more information, please see rightoncrime.com

Book prepared for publication by David Reaboi

Contents

Introduction

Dianna Muldrow
Texas Public Policy Foundation

Texas has incredibly high incarceration rates compared to other states. The huge numbers consistently cost taxpayers millions every year, as well as creating significant impacts on the economic environment in the state. Although conservative criminal justice reform has accomplished substantial decreases in these numbers in the last several years, Texas still has one of the highest incarceration rates of any state. Further efforts to combat this are occurring across the state in many different forums.

In December of 2014 professionals from across the board gathered in Harris County to discuss and answer questions about two pressing issues the criminal justice system is facing: pretrial release decisions and mental health. Assembled by the Texas Public Policy Foundation, they called for greater investment in risk assessments that make smarter decisions about pretrial release, and a "humane alternative" for mental health through collaboration.

Pretrial release decisions and a coherent response to mental health are both very important to criminal justice reform in different but inestimable ways. In the discussions that follow, pretrial decisions are all decisions from before arrest until a trial. Even considering the enormous numbers of people incarcerated in the state, there are also huge numbers of individuals cycling through the jail system every day. This has incredible impacts on employment and law enforcement resources.

Likewise, individuals who have mental health problems also have a complex relationship with the criminal justice system. An arrest after an offense will land them in jail, but often only for a very short amount of time, and after their release they will continue to have the same problems as before. Without any sort of intervention these individuals are condemned to repeated stints in jail, while exposing the general public to their later offenses, and wasting enforcement resources on a recurring issue that in no way deals with the problem at hand. With these situations in mind, these professionals called for various innovations in their field to prevent further inefficiencies and injustices.

Marc Levin began and moderated the discussion by noting the challenge that these issues present, and the success that Harris County is already seeing due to some of its initiatives. Crime has decreased, but he argues that if we want to lower it further and increase safety and well being, we need to identify areas of inefficiency and focus there. Levin then introduced the first speaker, David LaBahn, from the Association of Prosecuting Attorneys.

Admitting that his organization mainly works with larger offices, LaBahn acknowledged the time and resources necessary to take on these issues and find solutions. He urged both sides of the aisle to review and evaluate what has been done in these areas with an idea toward improvement. Having chosen Harris County as a pilot for the Smart Prosecution Project with his organization, LaBahn spoke about the potential in new reforms. Shifting focus from pretrial motions to pretrial releases through the use of risk assessments is one of these reforms, he argued. Following that up, needs assessments are pertinent to ensuring that you have the right people for the right reasons.

LaBahn closed with an anecdote that demonstrated the complex situation with medical expenses in the criminal justice system. The numbers show that reform for mental health is necessary, but they need a human reasonable alternative for this to be reached. In his opinion, jails and custodial facilities are not the place to have medical treatment.

Pretrial Panel

The morning panel consisted of Harris County Sheriff Adrian Garcia, Matt Alsdorf from the Laura and John Arnold Foundation, Tara Boh Klute from the Kentucky Pretrial Program, Judge Ryan Patrick and District Attorney Devon Anderson. They were gathered to discuss the current situation in pretrial, as well as ongoing and potential reforms.

Sheriff Garcia began by stressing the importance of this dialogue and its effect on public safety. Having already decreased the Harris County jail population by over a thousand, he agreed that continued successes would have to be achieved by refining and improving inefficiencies. Risk assessment and bonding schedules are clearly helpful tools that he argues will help bring this about. The Earned Early Release Credit is currently being applied to low-risk inmates, and has proven to be a success. Overall, he urged new methods that put former inmates on a trajectory to a more productive direction. This would result in fewer victims and expended resources.

Matt Alsdorf, the Director of the Criminal Justice Programs at the Arnold Foundation, followed Sheriff Garcia. He echoed the calls for risk assessments, and detailed a pretrial risk assessment that he and his organization had pioneered, that addresses the current conflicts being had with others. Tara Boh Klute provided information as well, on the pretrial programs that she and others have instituted in Kentucky. The lowered costs and supervision necessary bodes well for such reforms in Houston.

Judge Ryan Patrick and District Attorney Devon Anderson provided different outlooks. Judge Patrick brought out that while crime is down in Harris County, dockets are still overcrowded. A new court in Harris County could go a long way to addressing the backlog and allowing new methods to be instituted. DA Anderson remarked on the program currently being used for low risk marijuana offenders that involves less expense and has been a resounding success. Her objective is to keep from creating "classes of people who are sucked into the criminal justice system [forever]."

Mental Health Panel

In the afternoon a panel that included involved parties and stakeholders discussed mental health. Michael Dirden, the Executive Assistant to the Chief of Police, Dr. Teresa May, the Director of the Harris County Community Supervision and Corrections Department, Clarissa Stephens Deputy Director, Harris County Office of Criminal Justice Coordination, Dr. Andy Keller, from the Meadows Mental Health Policy Institute, all gathered to find solutions.

Dirden began by stating the problem; lack of capacity. Without room or alternatives in which to place those with mental illness, all the training in the world won't be helpful. Dr. May helped put that in context, by discussing the revolving door that this created, wasting resources. She urged the use of risk assessments for the mentally ill in order to best place them.

Stephens highlighted the difficulty that exists in agency education when the system is as vast and varied as Harris County. Dr. Keller agreed and argued that the real hang-up in taking programs to scale in the county is the individualized attitudes among agencies.

Judge Oscar Hale and Senator John Whitmire added to the discussion by touching on several other topics. Hale brought out the drug court education in schools program that he is involved in, and the revolving door that makes this necessary. But the drug courts that he and others are now involved in have really been making a difference. Whitmire echoed Keller by advocating interagency communication and collaboration. He emphasized that simply sending someone to prison is the easy option, but that alternatively treatment will provide better results by closing down the revolving door.

The theme throughout the day was collaboration. Risk assessments are being developed in many different ways and can and should be a new component of the system. A system that has improved is to be praised, but a system that continues down that path is a beacon and example to other jurisdictions and even states.

Where We Stand

WELCOME: Brooke Rollins
President and CEO, Texas Public Policy Foundation

We are so glad that you have joined us this morning, and are so grateful that you are here. This really marks a first for us at the Texas Public Policy Foundation—to provide a forum for discussing the big challenges facing the criminal justice system here in Harris County.

My name is Brooke Rollins and I have had the great blessing of leading the Texas Public Policy Foundation for the last twelve years. When I look back over the last decade and think about all of the different issues that we have worked on and put forward in Texas, the one that is closest to my heart is our criminal justice work. We have changed the conversation on criminal justice in Texas and thirty-five other states, and the message really rings true.

I want to especially thank our partners today, the Laura and John Arnold Foundation. Laura, John, their president Denis Calabrese, and their entire staff are real visionaries who make a difference. It is a privilege and an honor to be able to partner with them as we move forward; we are so excited that you are here. We are grateful that you have taken your Friday to affect and better tens of thousands of lives.

A few years ago the Texas Public Policy Foundation really only focused on a few key areas, taxes and education. We did a little health care, and a bit of tort reform—but had never thought of criminal justice reform. Then I began talking to one of our board members about it, and they thought that this was an incredible arena with potential for real change. We just needed to find the right person to head that up, and immediately I thought of one of the smartest, most dedicated, most entrepreneurial people that I've ever known, Marc Levin. I called him that day and asked him to think about joining TPPF and focusing on criminal justice. Barely pausing, he said, "I'm in!" Over the last eight years, he has done extraordinary things. Just this last year, he was named one of Politico's fifty greatest thinkers in the country. Please help me welcome the Director of the Center for Effective Justice, Marc Levin.

INTRODUCTION: Marc Levin
Director, Center for Effective Justice, Texas Public Policy Foundation
Policy Director, Right on Crime

One of the things that are so exciting about this work is that it brings people from across the spectrum together. I was testifying before Congress several months ago at a hearing about solitary confinement, and I was introduced to the ranking member of that Senate subcommittee, Dick Durbin from Illinois. He told me, "You're going to get us both in trouble for agreeing so much on things." And I said, "Well, look, I'm pleased to be here and I've known and admired the ranking member, Senator Cruz, who actually started our [Texas Public Policy Foundation] 10th Amendment Center for years." And Chairman Durbin jumped in and said, "Well, now you found something on which we disagree." Anyway, thank you all so much for coming I really appreciate it.

The issues that we will be discussing today we have focused on for years, though we haven't devoted quite the bandwidth we have given to prison systems at the state level. Frankly, though, this is a more challenging issue. Not only does this issue affect so many people, but it also has a serious effect on employment, housing, and families. Research has shown that by being in jail for twenty-four, or forty-eight, or seventy-two hours, can be enough to lose a job. By the same token, we need county jail. People that are in the middle of a crime spree need to be segregated from society. However, the high volume of people churning through the system creates a lot of challenges.

We are pleased that Harris County has made so much progress, along with other jurisdictions across the state, in addressing many of these issues. A good example of this is the mental health pilot program going forward under Senate Bill 1185, passed last session by Texas State Senators Huffman and Whitmire. We will get an update on that today from Clarissa Stevens with the Harris County Criminal Justice Coordinators Office. There is also the new marijuana diversion program that Sheriff Garcia and Devon Anderson have worked together to create, in addition to the mental health court, the veterans' court, and probation dual diagnosis beds. There are many positive initiatives going on here, and we have an opportunity to build on that.

Most importantly, though, the crime rate here in Texas' largest city is down. In Houston, crime has fallen by 19.6 percent since 2005. Murder is down by a third since 2005, and arson is down by half. Certainly there is always more to be done, but if we want to further reduce crime and further benefit taxpayers in terms of controlling costs, we have to make sure victims are empowered and receive the assistance that they need. Today we'll have an opportunity to explore some of these challenges and to identify some of the solutions in this area.

At the state level we want to get feedback from stakeholders in Harris County about goals for the legislature next session. I was speaking with somebody yesterday about being able to offer deferred adjudication for first time DWI offenders. This is to incentivize them to choose county jail over probation. When they do that, they get out with three for one pretty quickly. There is no interlock, no supervision, so you aren't addressing the alcoholism and it is much more costly for taxpayers. There are things that we know we can do on the state level.

Another example is the mental health issues. There was an increase in mental health treatment funding last session. One of the things that we want to be able to do for the next legislature is to make sure that we can show results for this. The Department of State Health Services is in sunset review, so that bill will be an opportunity to make further progress on these issues. We also have to look at other aspects of government, social services and the mental health system. There needs to be solutions across the spectrum, not just silos. Oftentimes, the county jail in the criminal justice system is the backstop only when everything else fails.

I'm pleased that we have a tremendous speaker here today to kick off this event. Dave LaBahn is the president and CEO of the Association of Prosecuting Attorneys, and has really been a leader in these issues. His organization has done a great job of putting on trainings for prosecutors across the country and even holding forums for prosecutors across the world, in order to explore how to be more innovative and effective in prosecution.

Previously, Mr. LaBahn was director of the American Prosecutors Research Institute and director of research for the National District Attorneys Association. Prior to that he was executive director of the California District Attorneys' Association. Before even that he was a very effective prosecutor in Orange and Humboldt Counties, in California. He's received many awards, including those for his work in combatting gang violence and assisting victims of crime. Please join me in welcoming Dave LaBahn.

Dave LaBahn
President and CEO, Association of Prosecuting Attorneys

At the Association of Prosecuting Attorneys, our mission is to work with prosecutors to make them more effective in reducing violence in the community. For my part, I've had ten years in the courtroom, ten years running a state association, and now eight years working at the national level.

One of the reasons that I moved around a bit is that nothing ever changes. I started in the Orange County DA's office. Some of you will remember that in the 1990s, Orange County went bankrupt. It wasn't the DA's office, or the prosecutors, or even the sheriff that bankrupted the county—it was the treasurer and, of course, we prosecuted him for it.

As an association, the Association of Prosecuting Attorneys is primarily comprised of larger offices. It isn't that small prosecutors' offices are not doing great things, or that they don't have an interest in reform; it's that the large office have the time and resources to engage in the dialogue and figure out how we can do things better. They are asking how we can make sure that we have safe communities and at the same time lower the incarceration rate. They ask if the treatment is really providing results. They can ask if we have caused more harm than good by putting someone through the system. If we aren't improving folks and they continue to be repeat offenders, have we improved our community? Or are we just further expanding the criminal population?

I want to commend Marc Levin and the Texas Public Policy Foundation. When you talk about reforms in California as compared to reforms in Texas, California just doesn't have the same popular appeal.

When you look at today's panels you have two very different topics on your agenda. One is pretrial justice, and the other is how to improve your mental health system. These are tough topics, and you are incredibly timely on them. But these are not easy issues and you have already put a significant amount of resources toward them, so I think is toing to be a very active dialogue to figure out how to improve and move forward. The fact that this event was sold out though shows how much interest there is, and already my discussions this morning have been very productive.

I really like that the Texas Public Policy Foundation is a conservative group that has made criminal justice reform a center-right issue. It shouldn't always be the left talking about what the criminal justice reforms should be; we need both sides to be part of the conversation. We can't always use what we've always done. We need to evaluate, test things, change things that need to be changed.

Harris was one of the four counties that were selected nationally in our Smart Prosecution project. The county's program, the Survivors Acquiring Freedom and Empowerment (SAFE) Court, is great. Harris is going to be an example as we push this nationally. We need to discuss what we are doing with young prostitution cases, especially first-time offenders. We need to know what is going on there, is it human trafficking? I'm not talking about smuggling; I'm talking about human trafficking. What is happening in your communities? Are you paying attention to who is really the victim in particular cases? We look forward to working with her office, because that is one of the areas that could very much move forward and change.

Now let's talk about pretrial justice. If any of the practitioners in the room where asked, "What's going on with pretrial?" they aren't going to think about bail decisions or release, they are going to think about their pretrial motions.

They will think about what they are filing and how they are responding to it.

Instead, we are talking about releases. We are asking who should be released, on what conditions they should be released, and whether we can get them services? We want to know if they are a risk. Is there a way to address their needs and get them in touch with meaningful services that will reduce the likelihood that they need to be a resident at the sheriff's facility? We need to address what is keeping them from getting back out in the community. Can it be addressed while they are out of the system? Some people think that risk assessments are phony things, but what's the harm in having another tool? Insurance companies use them all the time, so do many other businesses. I don't want to replace the judgment of the court, but that isn't want risk assessments are doing. It is a great foundation tool to help make the right decision for the right reasons.

The Arnold Foundation has the numbers and the statistics, and they are working with a number of different offices. You can go on the web right now and see all of the release decisions, the type of offender released, and what resulted. It is all based upon statistics and numbers. There is always a risk. There is always the possibility that someone, upon release, is going to do something awful. For example, just recently, a prosecutor in Alaska was killed by an offender that had been released. There are downsides, and bad things can happen; but if you are trying to make the right decisions for the right reasons, that is the direction to go in.

There are other things that you can use the risk assessments for besides release decisions. The Milwaukee district attorney is my board chair. They use the same risk assessments for their diversions. If you are going to look at alternative programs and try to keep cases out of the system, why don't you use that same risk assessment for that kind of a decision? I had a discussion with the Nashville sheriff and asked if they would be willing to share their risk tools with the DA in Nashville. They had already done the assessment, and it would help the DA on the diversion issues. The sheriff was more than pleased to help.

The next step is to have a needs assessment. I will point you to Portland,

Oregon, where the district attorney there is working very hard to recognize and address needs. We need to have the right folks in the system for the right reasons. It helps in disposition, it helps with alternatives and in that state there is state money involved. I can tell you about different areas in the country, but I need to know what works for you here, what have you already tried. If you don't try, you're never going to know what does and doesn't work. Collaboratively, looking at the panels in this conference and the way that they were designed, all of the different actors are presented here. They've come together to make good decisions and reform.

The second topic is asking what the right prescription for addressing mental health issues at arrest and beyond is. This is incredibly timely because, this past week, there was a national briefing by the National Association of Counties, and the Council of State Governments. It was a call to action on mental health, asking what we were going to do and what we could do better. In fact, Senator Cornyn was there at the congressional briefing, along with Senator Al Franken. How often do you see two senators that are philosophically polar opposites standing together and advocating a common cause? They were relying on their numbers, and they pointed out that the three largest jails in this country are, on any given night, housing 11,000 mentally ill offenders. State capacity, though, is 4000 beds. Prior to de-institutionalization in the 1980s, there used to be half a million beds. What has happened? Within one generation, we have moved people from state jails to county jails.

Miami-Dade County did a study that found that 97 of their repeat offenders cost the county $13 million within a span of three years. The Bexar County sheriff spoke and said that she is spending $2.2 million out of her budget on psychotropic medications. The Bexar County sheriff is saying that out of 4000 beds, 800 are occupied with those suffering from mental illness. One third of them have a serious condition. Is that what should be going on in jails? Is that the appropriate place for it? She has decided that she is going to screen every single arrestee. She wants to know why they had any involvement in the system at all. Since most arrestees are released, she believes that you are missing sixty percent of your population. That will be their strategy stepping forward.

Let's do a screen on the arrestees. Is there some place of treatment, or is there something that you can do? I've talked with your district attorney's office and you have mental health courts, you have crisis intervention teams, you have dedicated prosecutors and dedicated defenders, but what else could you do? Are there resources? It sounds like there needs to be a longer placement for people in crisis. Someone needs to watch them and make sure that they are taking their medication. The professionals in this room are the ones who are going to need to figure that out, but you need to look at your options. Can you look at other jurisdictions and see what they are doing?

Not to talk too much about your sheriff, but we have had conversations, and I know that, within the community of national sheriffs, there has been a very lively discussion about these issues. Even twenty years ago the medical costs were an issue for the county jails. The California system is very similar to the Texas system, with a county-based budget. I prosecuted what we called the Sheet Bandit, who was involved in a residential robbery that happened in Huntington Beach. Asian gangsters went into a house, pointed guns and then left in the homeowners vehicles. One of these individuals drove back to LA, and was pulled over by highway patrol. There was a standoff, and then the individual took off towards a hotel right by the University of Southern California campus. It created a huge potential hostage situation, but the guy tried to climb out of the window with tied together bed sheets. Unfortunately, he miscounted the needed number and couldn't make it down. In from of television helicopters, he let go and went crashing into the parking garage. He crushed all of the bones in his leg and went over to the USC medical center. We didn't serve a warrant on him until he rolled out, because if we did it before, then all of the medical costs would transfer from LA to Orange County.

Jails and custodial facilities are not the place to have medical treatment. Mental health is so incredibly expensive. Medications and supervision are so expensive. There has to be reasonable humane alternatives that can make a difference. I want to challenge all of you to do something, to make a change, and to make the community safer.

Pre-Trial Justice: Making the Right In-and-Out and Supervision Decisions

MODERATOR: Marc A. Levin
Director, Center for Effective Justice, Texas Public Policy Foundation
Policy Director, Right on Crime

Sheriff Adrian Garcia
Sheriff of Harris County, Texas

Thank you so very much and once again, thank you all for bringing us all together, and for all the great work that the Texas Public Policy Foundation and the Laura and John Arnold Foundation are doing to create a very, very important dialogue on public safety.

David LaBahn's comments earlier were really important, and they made me think about some of the initiatives that we have worked on. Since 2009 we have achieved over a hundred and twelve million dollars in operational savings within the sheriff's office. Coupling that with the fact that when I took office, we had a jail population that was eleven thousand four hundred at its peak, and now we are averaging about eighty-eight hundred. That has all been accomplished through respective initiatives. We tried electronic monitoring, which I still encourage judges to use in sentencing, despite the fact that it didn't go as well as we had expected.

He made some remarks about human trafficking, and it isn't often that government supports government, but I gave three hundred thousand dollars of my seized forfeiture to the juvenile detention center to start up a program to help those victims of human trafficking. Crisis intervention teams have been discussed since we started that particular program, and they have instituted about twenty-two hundred emergency and detention orders. They have effectively jail diverted over eight hundred people from the county jail. All of these things have contributed to the success that we are having in reducing the jail population, and add that with the fact that we have taken important steps in dealing with the prostitution population. We are lowering the demand instead of focusing on arrests of the women that I believe are principally the victims of prostitution. We instituted a program called Been There/Done That, started by a woman with a rags-to-riches story. She has walked the walk and suffered as a result, but pulled herself up by her bootstraps and is now an incredible life-changer for the women in our facility as well as the men.

It is my pleasure and always my honor to share the dais with our district attorney and I appreciate her leadership in all aspects and look forward to continuing to work with her, as well as the rest of these distinguished members.

I want to talk about the risk assessment and bonding schedule, as well as the recidivism study that was recently completed, and the idea of pretrial information sharing. There are important opportunities with the legislature coming into session. I think that risk assessment is good policy, and I think that having good reentry and providing good bonds helps equal good public safety. One of the things that we did to lower the jail population was institute an additional credit, we called it the Earned Early Release Credit. This was for inmates that worked on their education and got their GEDs and vocational certifications, as well as inmates that put in a good day's work. Obviously this only applied to the folks who are the least risk to the community, but if these groups play by the rules, work hard, do what we ask of them, then they get an extra day's credit for time served. This has had a significant impact.

The recidivism study that I mentioned has been looking for quantitative and effective measurement of particular programs. The Been There/Done That program, in two years, is averaging something like an eighty-five percent non-reoffend rate, which is phenomenal. It emphasizes the fact that if we put former inmates on a trajectory to a better and more productive direction, it results in fewer victims. It means less law enforcement and correctional services, as well as less prosecution services or resources expended.

All of this has to do with the fact that a significant portion of our population has a pretrial status. I have been advocating that we take a look at the way that we make decisions about who to give bonds to. Some argue that those that are in pretrial often have criminal histories, which I understand. But we have to look deeper, and evaluate whether there are any more bonding opportunities that we could provide. I believe that if we don't want to cause all of the residual effects of the current pattern, such as foreclosure, lost employment, and welfare, then we should handle the situation differently.

We need to make effective decisions in real time, it makes the overall system work much more effectively. For those of you not from Texas, you might not know that if you spend over twenty-nine days in my jail, your Medicaid is cancelled. Once you are released you have to have the skill set to reapply and re-qualify. A significant number of the people that this impacts are mentally ill and homeless, so it doesn't make a damn bit of sense. Since the purpose of the jail is to keep people safe, and we can accomplish this by getting offenders moving in a better direction, to have them leave the jail and be left to emergency rooms and patrol cars. This is wrong and doesn't make any sense because it isn't cost-effective. We need to look at that.

In closing, I'll say that while we have made a lot of progress, but we need to keep going. I use the term wild-ass ideas – "WAIs" – as the philosophy of my office. You have to be willing and have a bit of courage to try new things. We shouldn't be afraid of taking different bites of the apple, in order to get better results.

Matt Alsdorf
Director, Criminal Justice Programs, Laura and John Arnold Foundation

I'm really looking forward to talking to you today and having a discussion with the other panelists about how to make the best decisions about who really belongs in our jails and who can be safely managed in the community.

Before I speak about how the Laura and John Arnold Foundation has approached this issue, let me talk a bit about how we became involved in these questions in the first place, and why we believe it matters so much to public safety, cost effectiveness, and fairness. I joined the foundation about three and a half years ago with Anne Milgram, the former attorney general of the state of

New Jersey. Before that she was a prosecutor at the state, federal, and local levels. When we joined the foundation the board was looking to expand its role in the world of criminal justice, and we began working with them to identify the areas where the foundation could have the biggest impact. We are always thinking first and foremost about public safety, but we believe that making the best use of public resources and making sure that the system operates as fairly as possible enhances that goal. In our discussions with the board it didn't take too long to come to the conclusion that one of the areas that we should focus on was the front end of the system, which we decided was a broadly defined pretrial period. We included everything from arrest up until case disposition, where reform could make the biggest difference. Our thought was that if we were to make the right decisions, we needed to make them as early as possible. The challenge that we found was that a lot of the key decisions at the front end, such as who to detain, who to release, who to arrest in the first place, were being made by police, prosecutors, and judges that didn't have access to critical information and data. This information would assist them in determining whether someone poses a significant risk to public safety. This results in a significant number of low risk, non-violent defendants spending long periods behind bars before trial, and a surprising percentage of high risk and sometimes even violent defendants getting out quickly. We wanted to find a way to change the status quo to ensure that when judges make a decision about pretrial release or detention, they have access to a tool that provides objective data-driven information. This information would basically be a pretrial risk assessment, providing them with information about failure to appear risk that a defendant poses if released, but also the risk he will commit a new crime.

Currently only a small minority of jurisdictions uses this type of instrument, we have heard that it is less than ten percent. The main reason given for why there aren't more is that these tools cost money. The two reasons for this belief is that people believe that they aren't transferrable, that a risk assessment can't be done in Houston and then moved to Dallas, as well as the idea that each defendant needs to be interviewed. We wanted to cut out these costs by developing a risk assessment that could be effective and accurate anywhere in the country. There is more information about this on our site and I am happy to answer questions about it.

As a quick overview of what we've developed, the risk assessment is called the Public Safety Assessment Court. We developed it based on a large data set, about a million and a half cases from three hundred cities, counties, and all of the federal districts from across the country. Because the data set was so large and diverse we were able to look at an incredible range of risk factors, things like demographics, current offense, criminal history, employment, housing stability, etcetera. We tested hundreds of correlations between these risk factors and outcomes and identified the factors that are most predictive of each of these outcomes.

What we found is that with nine data points on any given defendant we could create a risk assessment that was equally predictive as existing tools and didn't require a defendant interview. Additionally, the tool would predict potential for violent offenses specifically. Our research was consistent with prior research that looked into these factors. We've also validated our findings in additional independent jurisdictions that didn't give us information the first time around. This is a very predictive tool across jurisdictions and regions about the three outcomes that we are concerned with; failure to appear, violence, and new crime.

We have piloted it across Kentucky for the last year and a half, and Tara will refer to some of the results that they have seen. I believe it has been a very powerful tool there, the pretrial crime has decreased since they began and the percentage of defendants released has increased. We are also piloting it in five counties in Arizona, California, and North Carolina and anticipate having data from these pilots in the spring of the coming year.

I also want to emphasize that risk assessments do not replace judicial discretion. There are two questions, what risk a defendant poses and what you do about it once that is assessed. The second question is still completely up to the judge. It remains up to the judge to determine, in each case, which risk mitigation strategies they want to impose.

Finally, we are also working on tools for prosecutors and beginning to look at some for police. We would like to be able to help guide their decisions so that they are more informed about the risks that a given defendant poses. When a cop is making a decision about whether to cite and release, or to arrest a defendant, he or she has information about their risk level. Likewise, prosecutors make a ton of crucial decision about charging, diversion, deferred prosecution, plea arrangements, recommendations to courts about release and detention, and we want to help with that. We are about to pilot a risk assessment for prosecutors that would help inform them in several jurisdictions.

Tara Boh Klute
General Manager, Division of Pretrial Services, Kentucky Court of Justice
Administrative Office of the Courts

I'm going to fly through this as quickly as I can and I'll be happy to answer any questions when we get to the discussion part. Really quick, Kentucky Pretrial has been around for a long time. We were created in 1976 as part of the Bail Bond Reform Act when commercial bail was abolished. In Kentucky, we have a statewide pretrial agency that is housed with the judicial branch of government, so we're actually in that third branch. We are with the administrative offices of the court, so we are a state agency. Our counties, the jails in the counties are run by the counties. Of course the counties love us because the state pays for us and everybody that we get released from jail, the county doesn't have to pay for, so it's a win-win for us.

There is two hundred and eighty-eight employees in Kentucky Pretrial Services, and over fifty programs in all hundred and twenty counties. We are a large program, but we don't cost very much. My entire budget to provide pretrial services for the entire state with two hundred and eighty-eight including me is only twelve million dollars.

We're able to provide pretrial services. We interview every defendant that is arrested and provide a risk assessment within twenty-four hours of that arrest and present it to a judge for a bail decision. When people are arrested, they don't have a preset bail unless there's a warrant. We speak to the judge within twenty-four hours and make sure that we get that decision very quickly. We do some investigation, supervisions, and diversion. I'm going to speak about the supervision before I show you the numbers. We intentionally don't supervise a lot of people because pretrial supervision is very taxing on our resources. We wouldn't be able to service all hundred and twenty counties if we supervised everybody. As it is, we supervise about ten percent of the released population, the highest risk defendants. We do get some orders where a judge puts conditions on lower risk individuals, but for the most part it is reserved to higher risk people.

I will give you an idea of our numbers. I pulled this data yesterday or the day before. We had two hundred and fifty-two thousand arrests in Kentucky last year, of which sixty-eight percent were given pretrial release. Of those sixty-eight percent released, almost sixty-five percent of them were released on recognizance. There was no bail involved, they were released on their own word. Of those that were given money bail, those were generally low bail amounts that the defendant was able to pay, and then it was returned when the case is over. There were about twenty-two percent that were unable to make bail. Their case was disposed of, but they said in jail for more than forty-eight hours. There was another seven percent that had their cases resolved within forty-eight hours. Finally, there is only three percent of that two hundred and fifty-two thousand that remain in jail now, awaiting trial, unable to make bail.

A majority of defendants in Kentucky are released pretrial. Looking at risk levels statewide, the lowest risk defendants get out eighty percent of the time. County by county there are some counties that have as meant as ninety-nine percent released, and some as low as forty. Only forty-four percent of high-risk defendants were released. In Kentucky, high risk means that eighty-four percent of those released are not charged with a new crime on pretrial release and about seventy-nine percent of them come back to court. It makes me ask, how high risk are these people? There are dangerous people that need to stay in jail, we don't want to let everyone out, but we do want to show how useful a tool pretrial release is.

Judge's discretion still factors into the decision. Someone who has been charged with a heinous crime may not have a criminal history, and rank as a very low-risk offender because of that. Judges still have the opportunity to detain that offender. They are required to look at evidence-based risk assessments, but that doesn't mean that they don't have discretion.

I also wanted to share with you some information about jail populations. Our pretrial jail population is right at forty percent capacity. To illustrate, where there a hundred beds in a jail, forty of them are held by pretrial defendants. The remaining sixty are either empty or have a sentenced inmate in them. Now, there are seven thousand and nine hundred defendants awaiting custody pretrial status in Kentucky jails. Our case processing is very quick in Kentucky, when someone is held in jail, unable to make bail, the average length of stay is only a hundred and nine days. If they are released, it is fifty-six. Defendants are moving rather quickly, and that is why we don't want to spend a lot of our resources supervising people. They are only with us for two months. This is why we reserve our resources for those higher risk defendants, because then we are able to get into every jail in Kentucky and have bail decisions within twenty-four hours to prevent people from languishing in the jails.

Judge Ryan Patrick
Judge, Texas 177th Criminal District Court

I'm going to take a little different tack regarding the pretrial side. I want to talk about the technology side of things, and the numbers that we use as judges to move cases more efficiently. I say this because I recently became chairman of what we call the JIMS executive committee. JIMS is the Justice Information Management System that is based on the 1970s mainframe technology. We are moving everything to sequel servers, so that it is a fully integrated system that will bring together off the shelf software packages in addition to anything that we build locally through our IT departments. It is a massive, multi-year, multi-million dollar project and I was lucky because when I got on the committee, it turns out that the felony district court judge is chairman of the committee, as well as the sheriff, the DA, and representatives from all of the different stakeholders. I'm not sure if this was purposeful, but having Kentucky as a comparison is very useful because the population between Harris County and Kentucky is fairly similar. We are dealing with comparable numbers.

When we look at pretrial and numbers of inmates coming through the system, it is important to think about the fact that there are twenty-two courts felony district courts here in Harris County. There are fifteen misdemeanor courts. The last district court that was added was Judge Ellis' court, the 351st, in 1985. The population of Harris County in 1985 was 2.7 million. We are now approaching 4.5 million. In the two short years that I've been on the bench, the average felony court docket has increased fifteen percent. In an average docket, about seven hundred and thirty cases, fifteen percent equals a hundred and five. My docket is actually down fifteen percent since I took the bench and I am still putting in effort to lessen the backlog, but that goes to show that while filings are flat numerically over the last couple of years, TDC population is down and projected to be flat by the legislative budget board. Deferred adjudications are flat. Considering the number of people coming to Texas, you can only deduct from that that crime is down. But since crime is down there is a disconnect, because our average dockets are climbing. My belief is that this has a lot to do with the CSI effect of our criminal courts.

There are more things that need to be tested and evaluated. DWIs are now strangling the dockets in misdemeanor courts, which is something that needs to be looked at. I think that it would be great to know what the cost benefit is, I've heard anywhere from a million to a million and a half would be involved in having a new district court in Harris County. What would be the benefit of adding a half a dozen felony district courts? What would that do to our overall numbers? Will that help reduce jail population? Will that move cases more efficiently? Two thirds of the entire Harris County jail population are felony pretrial inmates. Looking into those numbers deeper, it tells you that ninety percent of those have above the standard bond schedule for the charged crime. Something they have done has bumped their bond up higher. They are probably habitual or repeat offenders. This means that if they have committed crime A, which should have a bond of blank, their previous criminal history—or other aggravating factor—bumps the bond up. A lot of these people have probation revocations, and statutorily they have no right to a bond on probation revocation. There is a reason that they have higher bonds.

Some of the things that we are doing in Harris County are working very well. In fact, every morning, at 6 a.m. I get an email; we call it an orange sheet. That sheet contains the mental health and history of my new inmates. It includes everything that that person has touched, any contact that they have had with MHMRA, going back as far as the records can. We know right away what medications they are supposed to be on, what services they have had, or if they are missing something. If it is a drug case, are they self-medicating? Are they coherent for the defense attorney? If not, we need to get them stabilized and then return to the case when they are ready. That sheet makes sure that I have all of the data I need at my fingertips.

One of the other neat things we're doing, particularly through the JIM system is recently the contract was done for the new jail information management system, the new booking system. If we ever get to the joint processing center with the city of Houston, which provides 41% of the county inmates, then we're also looking at business processes. Why is it taking people longer to get to the risk assessment? Why is it longer for people to see a magistrate, to get a bond set? Well, because, you know, this, that and the other and here are the business processes. Well, they got to see medical. We don't want to release somebody who's going to have a heart attack on us. I get that. But now the technology, with the restrictions on business processes in technology, we're getting to the point where the technology is going to allow us to be so much more flexible. One of the other things coming back – and I'm running out of time, real briefly, when it comes to pretrial issues, anybody have any idea what one of the biggest speed bumps is we have now, one of the toughest nuts to crack on monitoring, particularly drug offenders or people we want to keep track of at their house? Phone lines.

One of the neat things that we are doing is the new booking system. If we ever get to the joint processing center for the city of Houston, then we're looking at business processes as well. We need to know why it is taking people longer to get to their risk assessment and why it takes longer for people to see a magistrate and get a bond set. Technology is going to make us much more flexible. For example, one of the most difficult things for us regarding monitoring today is phone lines. People don't have phone lines anymore, and if you have someone with an ignition air lock, that is $70 per month. If someone has an in home device, then that is a hundred, but it also requires a phone line. If you don't have a phone line - and I haven't in seven years – then you can get a radar device that you wear on your hip, which is a hundred and eighty bucks a month. If you want them to have the restricting device on their ankle that also requires a phone line, its seven bucks a month. A GPS system bumps it to eight. Technology is finally catching up to what we need to let people out pre-trial, but there is still a ways to go for it to be affordable.

Devon Anderson
District Attorney, Harris County, Texas

I want to talk about the pretrial marijuana program that we started a couple of months ago, because I think that it is the most relevant thing that our office is doing regarding pretrial issues. When I was in private practice, I had a large clientele of young drug offenders. As a judge over the drug court I noticed that young people picked up convictions very early, often because they couldn't make bail. They are charged with zero to two ounces of marijuana so that they plead to get out. I wanted to start a program where I would allow people who have never been in trouble before to have a chance to understand the severity of what they've done while not getting a criminal conviction at the end of the day.

So working with law enforcement—I did not do this in a vacuum—I talked to the sheriff, I talked to Chief McClelland, because those are our two biggest customers. They were whom I wanted to do the pilot with. I brought in Alex Bunin from the public defender's office to have the defense perspective, although I provide it myself, too. We worked this out. We did not use the cite and summons law, and I want to talk about why not. There were a couple of reasons. Frankly, one, we had seen what a disaster it was in Travis County, a forty percent no-show rate. The second was, I think the only way it will work is if we have mobile AFIS systems in every patrol car. The sheriff does, but HPD doesn't. The third problem was that the chief was telling me, so, Devon,

you want me to tell my guys that they've got somebody in custody with marijuana and that they're going to write a piece of paper, hand it to them, and they
still have to go tag the dope, they still have to go write a report, and they're
letting somebody stay where they were in the neighborhood where people who
live in the neighborhood don't want them there. That's not going to work. You
got to be able to take them away from the scene. Try dealing with all of these
concerns, which is what you have to do when you're making change, you have
to take into account existing infrastructure—that was the other problem, we
don't have a way to generate court dates. Yet, I'm not saying that none of this
can be fixed later. But I wanted to do something quickly. So we wanted to
work with what we had now. What we came up with was, I'm going to give
you an example, if an officer arrests somebody for zero to two ounces, class D
misdemeanor, marijuana, that's the pilot, and I may expand it later, if it's successful. So far, it's successful, too. That's why I was on my phone. I was making
sure it was, before I got up here.

If an officer takes someone into custody, they have to call DA intake to see
if there is probable cause. The officer is required to run down the facts to a
prosecutor, who will determine whether there is probable cause. If there isn't,
then we don't take the charge. If there is, they transport the offender to a sub-
station or to the closest fingerprint identification system. Once there they look
through the defendant's criminal history and AFIS them. We need to know
who we are dealing with and make sure they don't have out of state warrants or
are on probation, because I only allow first offenders who are charged with
marijuana in my program. If there is an unlicensed gun in the car with the
drugs, then they don't get in. If they have Xanax in the car with the marijuana,
they aren't getting in. Provided that they qualify, the officers briefly explain the
program to them and ask if they want to be involved. If they agree, then they
sign an acknowledgement form and are released with an assessment appointment scheduled for three days time.

At this point, I am happy to announce that everyone has shown up. I really
believe this to be because we know who we are dealing with. The transport and
fingerprinting show that this isn't just a traffic ticket that can be blown off, that
jail is a real possibility. These people don't want to go to jail, so they come to

the assessment. Most of them assess as low-risk, only a very small percentage are high risk. If they are low risk, then they have sixty days to do eight hours of community service. If they comply then the charge is never filed. If they assess at medium risk then they do an eight-hour cognitive class because they have some criminogenic factors. If they comply then charges are not filed. If they don't comply, then the DA's office files charges. We already went through the report and filing with the officers, so that is done.

This program increases public safety and quality of life. We aren't motivated by the money, instead we are trying to keep from creating classes of convicted people who are then sucked into the criminal justice system for the rest of their lives. But there are actual cost benefits. These people are never going to court. We have this program already instituted, it's been in effect for years in the juvenile division of our office, and it has an eighty-eight percent success rate. And that program isn't just for misdemeanors, it is for a lot of non-violent misdemeanor offenses. This is why, when I say that I want to expand the program, I mean that once we have opened it up to other agencies, and trained their officers, that I want to expand it to different offenses, like criminal trespass. Offenses that are low-level and non-violent.

The last thing that I want to say is that we are in the process of interviewing for a pretrial director. We want to get someone that is of the quality of Dr. May. We have three finalists interviewing in the next couple of weeks, and I think that you will see revolutionary change in the Harris County pretrial with the hiring of that director.

Q&A and Discussion

QUESTION: You spoke about people in the county jail having bail set at an amount higher than the schedule indicating that the offender has priors, making them higher risk. I'm not sure to what extent priors has been correlated with risk. My question is that—since your organization's research shows that priors are very important—are you supervising people who have a lot of priors? And would the risk assessment that you developed classify people as low or moderate risk even if they have priors?

TARA BOH KLUTE: Yes, we find that most people do have priors, but not significant ones. To be of the lowest risk, you would have a clean record, but you can still fall in the low risk range with a criminal history. You can have a prior felony conviction and/or a prior misdemeanor conviction. High risk usually mean there are multiple failure to appears, multiple violent criminal convictions, and a more serious records. However, there are people with pretty long records that still come out as low risk. We supervise people with all types of criminal histories.

QUESTION: I wanted to ask about the first chance intervention. I heard that you take booking photos and I wanted to know what was done with the pictures. I know that a lot of the trouble that people have later with employment and other things is that their picture is now online. Does that happen in this program?

DEVON ANDERSON: No, AFIS is run for identification purposes only, so there is no record that is kept. There will be an offense report kept by our office to prevent people from coming back consistently and getting in the program again. But that is the only record.

QUESTION: Judge Patrick, you mentioned adding more judges because of the workload. We've found that more judges doesn't always mean that they will do more work. I'm wondering if there is a way that you're going to monitor whether they are working more, or if you are just hoping that they will.

JUDGE RYAN PATRICK: I didn't have time to get into all of the details, but there are five of us working on a new docket management program. We are scheduling our cases completely differently than the way we have done it in Harris County from time in memoriam. Our benchmarks are time to disposition for certain levels of offenses. The goal is for eighty percent of your cases to be clear within six months to a year. We know that there will be about twenty percent that are a mess. My goal is also to get jury trials on the docket within a year, and with my newer cases, that has been successful.

I don't know what the correlation is between adding more courts and efficiency. That is one of the tricks here in Texas because everyone who is in the system, for the most part, is an individually elected official, an island unto ourselves. This means that we don't *have* to cooperate or collaborate with anybody. You are always going to have judges that work the hours they want to work and you will have some that don't. But our population dictates that we need more. We need to spread the workload.

QUESTION: Ms. Klute, you mentioned that pretrial doesn't supervise everyone, so how many are they supervising?

TARA BOH KLUTE: Of the hundred and seventy-one thousand that were released, seventeen thousand were referred to supervision and our active caseload as of yesterday was right under 6000 on supervised release. The remaining hundred and sixty-five thousand we still monitor for re-arrest and FTA.

QUESTION: The last question is for the DA. I commend you for that program. I think that is wonderful. Do the defendants pay anything to be part of that program?

DEVON ANDERSON: There's a hundred dollar fee that pays for the class, and if they can't afford it, we have an indigency program.

MARC LEVIN: I wanted to ask about indigent defense. As much as we try to involve everyone, we don't have a criminal defense lawyer speaking today, but some of the things that we've heard about quite a bit are issues involving people pleading to time served sometimes even if they didn't commit the offense, just to get out of jail. Oftentimes you might have a criminal defense lawyer who has an enormous docket and may not have the opportunity to fully investigate the facts of a particular matter. I wanted to kind of see if any panelists could comment on how strengthening indigent defense representation could help with some of the issues that we've been discussing today.

TARA BOH KLUTE: One of the pushes in Kentucky was to have a public defender at every arraignment. In Kentucky, the initial bail decision is done over the phone, there is no prosecutor present, there is no public defender present, it is a non-adversarial process. It is based on the defendant's charge, their risk assessment, and the recommendation of pre-trial. But if they don't make bail, then they are taken to jail arraignments. At that point we involve public defenders in all but one jurisdiction. Ed Monahan – our public advocate – can rattle off numbers on how the presence of the public defender affects the chances of the defendant.

JUDGE RYAN PATRICK: The only thing that I would add is that in Harris County, if you are in custody and indigent, once you notify the court, you get an attorney that day. But defense attorneys rarely ask for pretrial supervision. They might ask for the bond to be lowered, but they assume that they can't have pretrial supervision. Personally, I have found that pretrial personal bonds are much less likely to appear than commercial surety bonds. There is a gap somewhere in our assessments.

DAVE LABAHN: Judge, you spoke about the number of courts. My home county was Orange County, California, with about a 3.2 population. They have a hundred and twenty-four judicial positions and twenty additional court commissioners, with about sixty percent of them working criminal cases. The fact that you only have twenty-two shocks me, considering your population and your workload. That is where I wanted to go on the question with the defenders. This process takes time, and you need to slow the system down.

These alternatives don't mean that you still need to do a good job though. Milwaukee is a great example, because the prosecutors office diverted thirty percent of their cases, but then the state cut their size. It needs to be the other direction. We need resources, we need judges, we need prosecutors and defenders. If you invest in that on the front end then ultimately your jail costs and other things go down. But it is too shortsighted of the funding organization to cut funding because case-loads are down.

QUESTION: As a prosecutor, how are you balancing the risk evaluation with the type of case that you have? How would you handle, say, a high risk offender that is involved in a bad case?

DEVON ANDERSON: If we don't have a case, we don't have a case. That's the end of the discussion, public safety or not. We will do everything we can to build up a case, and make sure that we have one. If there's another charge that we could file, we could do it. When we have a dangerous person, it's very disturbing when you realize you can't prove the case beyond a reasonable doubt, but our oath is to seek justice and that's it. There are no ifs, ands, or buts about that. We have to get rid of the case.

QUESTION: I know that defense attorneys have balked at the criminogenic risk assessments in other communities across the country. There is a real friction between old school defense attorneys, who do we bring them along to see that this is good for their client?

JUDGE RYAN PATRICK: This is real world experience that happens too frequently in my court. To illustrate, say you have someone who is on probation for a drug case, and he goes through a nine month program that he wanted no part of. He wanted his back time and to be done with it, so I brought him out. He had a great defense attorney who asked me to bring him out and we read him the riot act. He was nineteen and didn't care, he just wanted his TDC back time and to be on his way.

The other bag of tricks we run into is this, an attorney may come up and say that their guy has an old record and they think that he needs treatment. They might want to do the assessment pre plea to see what it says. I've done that for them. I stopped doing it because too many were going on probation by recommendation, and the inmate was saying that he would prefer a year lockdown to the longer program. I can shove people into programs, but at some point, they all don't want treatment.

DR. TERESA MAY: Let me note that Judge Patrick isn't in my pilot yet. I'm Dr. May, I believe I've been mentioned today, but I'm the director for the probation department. The frustration that Judge Patrick is speaking of is the reason that we are redesigning how we do assessments in Harris County. We have three of his colleagues on the new process. It is an education process with the defense bar, but they don't understand that it is also a risk reduction/risk management plan. In addition to getting a good solid risk assessment, we are also screening for mental health and substance abuse. Right now I have three felony courts that have been doing that for about five months, and so far the feedback from the judges agrees with Judge Patrick, it is all about how we present the data, so if we make a recommendation for residential treatment or outpatient treatment.

Some of the feedback that I have from his colleagues is that the reports are balanced, fair, and clear. It is quick and easy to look at. It is an ongoing project, but it is doable. We are seeing real progress with it. We'll try to get Judge Patrick on our new pilot as soon as possible.

JUDGE RYAN PATRICK: I do the assessment post-plea pre-sentence, so I have them come back, but when I sentence them, I let them know, that here's what we're doing and if you're going to get this residentially, I'm going to follow that. Then sometimes they go, well, let me talk to my lawyer and we'll work something out. So sometimes we cut it off before we can even get that far.

DR. TERESA MAY: Right. It does. I've seen a few different things. One is the new process really is designed, you're going to get more quality than you're getting right now, because we actually have clinicians doing the substance abuse and mental health assessments. They're going to get at some things in combination with the risk assessment that are going to be more specific, and more helpful. Also they would have talked to the client a little bit more ahead of time, so I think that information will be helpful.

MATT ALSDORF: May I add something on the defense bar side? Some of the perception tends to be that whatever baseline we are at, and adding a risk assessment is only going to apply upward pressure. What we've seen in a lot of places is that if you take violence as a category, six or seven percent of defendants are flagged as being at an elevated risk of violence. The data that we've seen in Kentucky is that if they are released, they are seventeen or eighteen times as likely to commit violent acts. It is a small group of people that are flagged, and they are at a very elevated risk.

I think that it is important to emphasize that we care immensely about making sure that we are doing the most to protect the public from people who are high risk, but that isn't everyone. In fact, it is a very small percentage. In fact, in Kentucky, they have increased the percentage of defendants released, and decreased pretrial crime. The hypothesis would be that they are changing the mix of who is detained and detaining more high risk people. I think there is pretty good data to use in speaking with the defense bar about the impacts.

TARA BOH KLUTE: I want to add that the only issue that our public defender's office has had with anything that we've done is the elevated risk of violence flag. That is the only thing that they have had any issue with. They support everything else and it is just important to educate them on what it really means, as Matt said, it is a very small percentage of people who are actually flagged.

MARC LEVIN: One thing that I want to mention is that one of the bills that will be heard next session will allow someone who has completed two-thirds of their probation for a state jail felony to apply to have that reduced to a misdemeanor. It would have to be signed off on by the district attorney and the judge, but the idea is that a lot of state jail felons are choosing jail instead of probation, and that this would be an incentive for them to choose probation and be successful. I absolutely agree that someone has to be willing to do the treatment, but if we can provide an incentive, I think that will help.

QUESTION: I'm a brand new defense attorney, and I don't want to speak for the entire defense bar, so I apologize if I step on anybody's toes, but one of the issues that I've seen in some of my cases are that to do the risk assessment the cases have a lot of innocence issues as well as assessment issues. A lot of time the prosecutors and judges come from a mindset that everyone through the system is automatically guilty, but there is a lot of innocence claims in all of these cases, and you have to give that up for the risk assessment. There are a lot of rights that defendants have based off of those innocence claims. How do you ensure that you are protecting those innocence rights while still assessing risk and allowing someone to get the help that they need?

TARA BOH KLUTE: I think that has been some confusion about risk assessment. What we do in pretrial is for a bail decision. We would never ask information about a charge. We do not even speak to the defendant about their charges. The risk assessment that we use is very objective. The judge was referring to a probation risk needs assessment, where they look at criminogenic factors. The pretrial risk assessment has no criminogenic factors. I hope that clears that up a bit. We don't ask anything about the charge.

NICK WACHINSKI, *American Bail Coalition*: Colorado is a state that has been exploring risk assessment. In my last tenure this past session in Colorado

I was confronted by both the prosecutors, the bench, and the defense attorneys, suggesting that the criminogenic factors has been abused by certain prosecutors in negotiating or making plea offers. In fact, they say that if it is a higher-level score then they won't give you a pleas offer. So how do you address that? And my second question is how commercial bail fits into risk assessment.

JUDGE RYAN PATRICK: The only thing that I would say is that when it comes to commercial bail, my experience is that they, or a loved one, has some real skin in the game. That is my experience. I don't have experience with non-commercial bail system, and I don't give a ton of personal bonds. Their track record is pretty poor, it is a whole system that needs to be looked at, particularly here in Harris County.

DEVON ANDERSON: I'm in the dark about what a risk assessment for bail would look like, but I know that when we are crafting a plea bargain offer, we are looking at what the person has done and we are looking at what they have done in the past. It is being examined from a public safety standpoint. We want to know if they need drug treatment, and can we rely on them to not hurt anyone. If we think that they are a danger, we offer pen time. I don't think that there is anything wrong with that.

JUDGE RYAN PATRICK: Sometimes I'm presented with teenagers that have no money, they're in school, finals are in two weeks, and I have to look at whether they have a stable place to stay, if they have any support, do they have a history with mental illness and if so, who are they being treated? I need to know if they are going to be able to make it back to court. I've taken chances, but the track record has been poor.

MATT ALSDORF: Nick, we haven't articulated a position about this, but we have worked in places that don't have commercial bail, and places where they do. We have used our risk assessment in both areas. We go with the jurisdiction and they use their toolbox and we work with them to overlay the risk assessment with that existing toolbox.

The Right Prescription for Addressing Mental Health Issues at Arrest and Beyond

MODERATOR: Hon. Jerry Madden
Former Chairman, Texas House Committee on Corrections

Michael Dirden
Executive Assistant Chief of Police, Houston Police Department

On behalf of Police Chief McClelland and Mayor Parker, I want to thank all of you for inviting the Houston Police Department to participate in this, but I also want to apologize in advance. Normally, we don't wear our dress uniforms to events, but unfortunately we have a funeral for a law enforcement officer at about eleven o'clock and I will be attending that later.

I think it's really, really important to mention that from the perspective of the Houston Police Department, the real star of our effort to work with folks who are suffering from mental illness and develop compassionate and appropriate response to this issue is a very good friend of mine, a person that I work with on a daily basis. It is Captain Wendy Bainbridge and I'm going to ask Wendy to stand up. She's not going to want to stand up. Wendy will be available for questions if you need someone to expound on what we're doing and why we're doing it.

From the perspective of the Houston Police Department, a local law enforcement agency that is committed to this process, the single biggest issue for us with respect to dealing compassionately with folks who suffer from mental illness is the lack of bed space in Harris County, a problem not only in Harris County, but also throughout the state. This is the most prevalent issue for us because, despite our shining example on refining law enforcement from the blunt instrument that it used to be, unfortunately, when there is a lack of capacity in the overall system, there isn't bed space or professionals who can respond. In a number of cases, you still have law enforcement acting as the primary response to persons who are suffering crisis. Many of us, despite our training, are not well equipped to handle that. Most importantly, though, when we do address a situation and are capable of handling it in a manner that is compassionate and consistent with human dignity, if we don't have anywhere to take them, the alternative is to take them to jail.

Now, since 2004, our response protocol allows us to have over a thousand officers who are trained in crisis intervention training. In addition to that, our dispatchers are trained to try to recognize call for service slips that are focused on individuals who may be suffering from mental crisis, which allows us to get the appropriate persons there. We created a mental health division where we have dedicated officers who are assigned, when possible, to handle the bulk of those calls. If there's a call for service involving a person with mental crisis, we try to get somebody there who has training and experience and education and a demonstrated ability to exercise compassion. We try to get someone trained to respond to those situations.

But here's the rub. Last year we had 30,000 calls for persons who were either in a mental crisis or situations related to mental illness. We do have a chronic consumer stabilization program that is assigned to the mental health division where we have officers and MHMR clinicians that we team up and we try to get them to the scene of these incidents so they can assist in handling these incidents in a compassionate and humanistic manner, but there are only twenty-four of those. Thirty thousand calls for service, only twenty-four people. The Harris County Neuropsychiatric Center is full most of the time. It's on drive by on a daily basis, and that is not their fault. That's a lack of capacity in the system. Even when we get trained personnel to the scene, we don't have anywhere to take them, other than to a jail. We all will hear from folks who represent the jail staff in Harris County later, they do an excellent job over there, but they're stretched to capacity.

So from the perspective of the Houston Police Department, our number one goal is to try to assist all of the stakeholders in this to increase the capacity for bed space, outpatient centers, and training for law enforcement officers across the state that we need in order to provide humanistic services to a population that is severely in need. It is important for us and we stress all the time to our police officers that people don't call the police all the time because they want to see the police. People call the police. Have you ever wondered why firemen are really, really, really loved and police are not very liked very well? Because when you call the firemen, they come and they do what? They put out the fire.

They're either going to put out the fire or bring you medical attention. You call the police because it's the only other agency that's open on a twenty-four hour basis and we have told the community for a hundred thousand years, that if you call us, we will come. But relief from the problem causing the call takes longer than from a fire. But we've set up this artificial evaluation in the system that talks about police response time. "The police got there in less than five minutes, well, police response time is good." And that's the measure of the quality of our service, but that isn't the point. The measure of the quality of our service is not how fast we get there. The measure of the quality of our service is what we do when we get there.

When dealing with persons with mental illness and suffering from mental crisis, it's still the commitment of the Houston Police Department to provide the most humanistic services that we have. There are officers who are committed to getting there and making a real difference in how those persons are treated in the system, but also how they are treated by our officers. Most importantly, however, the best thing that you can do to help us is give us somewhere to take them, because taking them to jail is not a viable option.

Teresa May
Director, Harris County Community Supervision and Corrections Department

Carey Welebob, the director for TDCJC, which is our oversight agency for probation has worked really hard with us in the development of a new risk assessment tool. It was her leadership that really made this happen, and I want to make sure, if you haven't met Carey, that you talk to her because we are in the process of implementing a great new risk assessment tool. The risk assessment tools haven't changed in Texas for thirty years, and it's something you've heard a lot about today, because we're excited about it.

My job primarily, when it comes to pretrial jail, is to help people succeed once I get them. And my best impact on the jail is to make sure that I do everything I can to keep people from coming back in. We all know that there's a door, but it's a revolving door. When we look at people with mental illness – and I'm a licensed psychologist, so I've seen it all - I think it's important for everyone to understand that that population, just like everybody else, divides up into groups and that risk does matter. Not only do we have to look at the mental illness itself and understand what's going on with that person, we need to do our same risk assessments that we're doing on our regular probation clients and other individuals in the criminal justice system, on the mentally ill as well.

It is important to have them in a state where you can speak with them and help them understand, so that they can communicate with you and you can get valid information. These are some of the things that we work through with our mental health partners. It's important to understand that while getting those individuals medication is important, because these individuals are at higher risk to continue involvement in the criminal justice system. They need medication, but they also need intervention. So for those of you who don't know a lot about risk assessment, there are about seven things that consistently predict failure. Some of these indicators are the people that you are surrounded with, your family, your neighbors, and what is going on there. Is it stable, or frequently disrupted? Are there drug problems involved? Substance abuse is an issue. Criminal attitude is also an issue, how the individual thinks and reasons.

What the research shows us is that the mentally ill population in criminal justice really does divide out into groups. There are low risk individuals which I think Harris County and Captain Bainbridge have done a phenomenal job with and she needs more support from anybody in here that has money, because that is a phenomenal operation to redirect low level, lower risk individuals. They deal with some situations that are scary and do a phenomenal job, but an important thing they're doing on the front end is trying to divert low risk individuals that don't even need to enter the jail. They don't have a lot of resources; this group just doesn't have anywhere to go. There's another population that continues to revolve in and out that is substance addicted. They have drug problems, serious drug problems. They might have peers that are also in trouble, criminal trouble. They could have difficulty at home or a whole host of other factors that we have to focus on.

I've spent time really working with this population, and when I get these individuals, I want to know as quickly as possible what's going on with them mental health wise. I also want to know what the risk level is. I want to know how many criminogenic factors they have. What we know from the research is that the same things that predict re-arrest in our general probation and offender population predict re-arrest in the mentally ill population. So you have two vaults. You want to get their mental health issues addressed, but you need to address the drug problem and other issues as well. What I encounter are families that are exhausted. They've been trying everything they know at times. There are some people who don't have family. It's important that we target those issues, and that's what we focus on in probation. We need a timely assessment when we do get them. We want to identify mental health issues. We want to partner with our local mental health authority and try to get individuals treatment, which involves a lot of challenges because we're huge. This means that the system needs to adapt to the volume and the fact that criminal justice involved individuals are a bit different in what they need. We want to target those criminogenic risk factors. I'm going to leave it at that for right now because I think we can get to some other things as we do Q and A. But that's what our focus is when we get people on probation and we do have some great resources to do that.

Clarissa Stephens
Deputy Director, Harris County Office of Criminal Justice Coordination

There is so many good things going on in Harris County, but before I start I just want to remind everyone of how big Harris County is. The unincorporated area alone in Harris County is larger than the entire city of San Antonio, and then we have Houston sitting right in the middle of that. I wanted to build off of what Chief Dirden said. The sheriff's office does have nine

CIRT teams, and we have three more in the works. Another kind of preventative program that started in April of 2013 is the Houston Recovery Center, which Wendy knows a great deal about. They have admitted over eighty-seven hundred people since then – many of which have co-occurring disorders - that have been diverted from public intoxication charges.

What I want to talk about, though, is what happens in Harris County from the time a person does get arrested until their first court appearance, and just how we identify mentally ill people and how they move through the system. I will remind you that Harris County has over a hundred arresting agencies, which means that there are a lot of issues surrounding agency education. After charges are accepted and within a few hours of booking into the county jail, a person has a probable cause hearing. Probable cause hearings in Harris County happen twenty-four a day, seven days a week. At that time, a court is assigned and the next morning, if the person was booked by ten p.m., they're going to be in front of their home court. At booking, there are three chances to identify a mental health issue. The first is during the pretrial interview. The second is by the booking deputy, who uses a screening form for suicide and medical and mental impairment, which is then printed for the intake nurse if there are any affirmative answers. Before classification, each detainee, whether they're there on a new charge or are a parole violator or have a warrant from out of county, will go through the intake nurse. The intake nurse has been trained to ask questions that can identify mental health issues. In addition, the sheriff's office has a really robust EMR system and a mental health database that has mental health history in the jail back to 2001. That intake form is populated with any information that we have on mental health so that the nurse is aware of the individual's history. There are about 290 people that are booked into the Harris County jail everyday and an average of 55 of those are sent directly to the mental health clinic, before they go to classification. That's about 22 percent of the people that are booked into the jail. On Wednesday, there were 8,488 people in the jail and 2,212 of those were on psychotropic meds.

We do a really good job of identifying people and getting treatment started that night, as soon as they're booked into the jail. Our jail has 296 beds for acute and sub-acute mental health needs and provide group therapy in those units, targeting psycho-educational skills, substance use, and wellness recovery. Another thing the sheriff has done to help with continuity of care in 2012 is a process that provides persons without an ID with a picture former inmate ID card that's recognized by Harris Health, MHMRA, the Houston Council on Drugs and Alcohol, the AIDS Foundation and numerous area shelters. It's also accepted by DPS as a secondary identification for obtaining a Texas ID. This year, to date, 675 of those have been printed and issued as people leave. Also, the health care for the homeless jail in reach program began in 2007, and has served over 1700 mental ill homeless individuals and successfully linked over 1100 of those to services.

Judge Patrick also mentioned the orange sheets. What happens with those is that every night at midnight, there is a match between MHMRA's Anasazi system and the mental health database in the jail. If a new person has been booked into the jail and is identified, then Anasazi sends diagnosis information to the sheriff's office. When the dockets are created, I think at around two o'clock in the morning, there are electronic orange sheets that are created for everyone on a docket that has the information that he mentioned. In addition to that, there is also a list of people that are in jail that are on medications so that the sheriff's office can make sure they get their dosage before the individuals in question go to court so that no medications are missed. Finally there is also an algorithm that is performed for the Public Defender's office that identifies high needs indigent individuals that they will be able to represent that day in the misdemeanor courts. On Wednesday, there were two hundred and fifteen of those orange sheets created for our courts.

Both the public defender and the DA's office have mental health divisions and - this year - the public defender sponsored a series of CLE events for defense attorneys and prosecutors that wanted to obtain additional expertise in mental health. Throughout that series, there were three hundred attendees, twenty-one people that attended seventy-five percent or more of the series took a test and passed it. That gave them a designation of competency in representing mentally ill clients and those have been flagged on the appointment list. The district attorney's mental health division has five lawyers, one investigator, one paralegal, and one assistant. They work primarily in the felony courts. They have plans to train the fifteen misdemeanor chiefs and hire a felony chief prosecutor to help all the chiefs recognize mental health issues and whether or not to call in the mental health division. The public defender has five misdemeanor lawyers with plans to add two next year and two felony lawyers with plans to add one. There are two investigators and two social workers in their mental health division.

Harris County has quite a few specialty courts, and all of these have people in them that have a mental health issues. We do have two felony mental health courts since April of 2012. There have been over two hundred and fifty referrals and a hundred and three participants, and all of those met the criteria for Texas priority populations. Diagnoses in eighty percent also met criteria for co-occurring substance disorders. I don't think that we have talked enough about how we need to combine all of these interventions, mental health, substance abuse, and physical health. They generally all roll together and we need to find a way to blend interventions appropriately. There are also two district critical time intervention mental health court dockets for people on probation that are at risk of revocation. There are fifty-four people on those dockets. There is also a competency restoration docket for people that are in the process of being restored or are incompetent and unlikely to restore. Currently that docket has two hundred and eleven people and about half of them are even in a facility on recommitment, in a facility waiting to be restored or awaiting placement. Since that docket was established, five hundred and ninety people have been restored.

I know everybody's interested in hearing what's going on with the jail diversion – mental health jail diversion pilot, affectionately known as SB-1185. We have identified over three thousand people that have had three or more bookings in the last two years that meet the qualifications for that program. On a real time basis, we match that list with people that are in jail and provide Dr. Hicks, who is the director of that program with that – she has access to that list at all times and they use that list for referrals in the jail. At this point there have been anywhere from four hundred and fifty to five hundred people that are in the jail at any given time out of that three thousand. Currently, they have ninety-seven people enrolled. Fifty-four percent were enrolled while they were incarcerated. Those are people that have already completed their cases and they were screened and wanted to be in the program. Twenty-two percent are referrals from the community at large and another twenty-five percent were referred by MHMRA as current clients that needed that extra, extra help. There is currently three county criminal courts that are participating in a pilot with that program. My time is up, but I'll be happy to answer any questions.

Andrew Keller

Executive Vice President for Policy and Programs,
Meadows Mental Health Policy Institute

I need to tell you that, you know one thing I can do as a new Texan is I can talk like a Texan, comparing Texas to the rest of the country and maybe I can get some credibility because you don't have credibility when it's your hometown. You know, you got credibility when you come from outside. I'm still coming from outside. I'll tell you, from outside you all have the cornerstones and foundation laid in Harris County and to some degree in Texas to have successful full-scale diversion, more than I think any other state in the country. The people that you have here, that you have here in Harris County are among the top leaders, the top people doing research on risk assessment. Teresa is here. You've got a DA who is friendly, you've got judges like Judge Patrick. You've got the people here to do the best job in the country with diversion. Sheriff Garcia, one of the very first people I talked to when we were forming the institute to say, "What do we need to do around mental health?" Chief Dirden is running state of the art national best practice intervention crisis teams. So clearly, the problem about bringing things to scale is not in your correctional systems.

Now I need my friends in the mental health system to cover their ears for a second. The problem is in the mental health system. And I'm here to say it's the mental health system. It is not the individuals here. You have some of the best people in the country working here in Harris County. The awesome Dr. Shah at Harris Health, Rose Childs and Dr. Knox at MHMRA, You've got outstanding individuals, state of the art practices, and the 1185 project that's going on. You have some wonderful partnerships and a lot of people like to say that the system is broken, have you ever heard that one? That the system is broken? This is one of my least favorite sayings because I don't remember the time that the system was not broken. Once there was this time where we dropped the system, it shattered and it became what it is today.

We never actually got the system working, so when I say that the mental health system is not working, it isn't because people are doing things wrong, it is because we haven't figured it out yet. What we are trying to figure out is what the strengths and opportunities are within the system and what areas we need to improve upon to move forward. We think this is one of the big areas. It's not because you're doing worse here than in other parts of the country. You might be doing better than most places in the country. It's just that none of us are doing a particularly good job. So how do we improve? How do we get a framework for this? First, instead of thinking about what new program we could use to incrementally take the diversion program to scale, we should focus on actually taking it fully to scale.

How do we sort of shift our vision from just adding another court, adding another CIRT, adding more slots? When Clarissa spoke before about the new 1185 program, she was speaking of about ten percent of the population. If I did the math right, it's going to serve about ten percent of the people that you've got there. That means there is about ninety percent of the people that may have these needs that we're not going to be able to serve. Chief Dirden spoke about how the Neuropsychiatric Center is a state of the art model. It's right there at Harris Health, it's right by the hospital. It's co-located really. It's got all the great features, but most days, as he says, it's on diversion. You're diverting thousands of people a year through that. So how do we take things to scale?

The answer isn't just building more beds. Like Chief Dirden said, it's having more capacity. Building beds isn't the answer because you've maybe about a hundred or two hundred new psychiatric beds coming in to your community, and you may have added some over the last year, and you're going to be adding more. Clearly simply adding beds isn't the answer. It isn't simply giving more money either. I mean, I'm not going to say money is not important. My boss

Tom Luce likes to say that funding is not irrelevant. I think that is an excellent way to talk about funding. You don't want to lead with that, but it certainly is not irrelevant. But it isn't the answer in itself. You have had a hundred and twenty million dollars more today being spent on an annual basis on mental health in Harris County than you did two years ago. Did you notice that? Did you notice a hundred and ten million dollars more of impact in terms of reducing needs? My guess is you probably noticed some, but you're not noticing that much.

It's not a lack of the right people, so what is the issue? I think that the thing that is lacking is a systemic perspective. The problem is that there are system barriers here. I want to talk about just three of them, one of which was talked about earlier by Sheriff Garcia. This is the suspension of Medicaid benefits. I'm not going to get up here and tell you that we need to do more Medicaid in Texas. If someone asks me a question, I will expound upon my thoughts, but what I will say is that if we are going to give someone Medicaid, the least we could do is let them keep it if they get in trouble and not make them go through all of these hoops again. It is a waste of resources to make these folks go through that again. We should allow Medicaid benefits to be suspended, for a reasonable amount of time. We'd like them to be eligible when they come out because we want to keep them out. That is a very minor change that would help.

The second one is a little bit harder, but I think we can do it this year. It's performance metrics. Right now, there are no meaningful performance metrics related to diversion in the mental health system, but there are opportunities to create them. The Sunset commission passed DSHS recommendation 2.3, calling for a comprehensive review over the next two years of the performance metrics related to mental health. HHSC, Sunset report that was just voted unanimously earlier this week in 6.1, was recommendations that my boss, Mr. Luce, who's on the commission, put forward. It requires HHSC to align its metrics, particularly around crisis intervention for the LMHAs, but also for the district projects, the 1115 waiver projects. That's where that hundred and twenty million dollars came from, as well as for the Medicaid MCOs. We don't talk a lot about Medicaid MCOs, but the Medicaid system serves more

Texans with serious mental illness than the local mental health authority system. Your MHMRA serves a lot of people, does great work, but statewide – and I don't know how this parses out exactly for Harris County, but the statistics are probably as true here as anywhere in the state - more people with a serious mental illness are served through your Medicaid MCOs.

How do we get these systems where we're spending hundreds and hundreds of millions of dollars every year to actually work together and to come together around performance metrics in behavioral health? And what do I mean by performance metrics? I mean the things that Clarissa and Dr. May were talking about. You get a tremendous amount of data here in Harris County. You know of the vast majority of people who have mental health needs who come through your system. What we need to do is we need to boil that down to some metrics. Let me give you an example of what we would do with that. We're working right now in Bexar County with the justice center, with Tony Fabelo, and the folks at the Council of State Governments on a jail diversion pilot there where the aspiration is to go system-wide and have a hundred percent of folks who can be diverted, diverted. What we're doing is we're taking a little bit more robust of a screening tool than what you're using right now here. It's not just suicide risks, it looks at some other things. It isn't as robust as the assessments that Dr. May's group does; it is sort of in between. It's a screening tool that has more information and we're using that and crossing it with the T-RAS against risk. Then we're identifying groups of folks and we're trying to slot them, then, into different types of diversion. If we could identify all those folks and have a metric for that, guess what? You could hold your system accountable for it. That sounds like a little thing, but it's a little thing that could be a really powerful lever to start moving people. Everybody's going to say that the data isn't reliable. Well, of course, it's not perfect, but do you know what makes systems more reliable? Using them. You start using data, people get really good at it and of course they game it, of course they do, we're human beings. But people game all systems, they do that all the time, so we have to better calibrate, have better incentives and oversight. But this data is probably one of our most important opportunities.

That brings us then to the third reform, which is something you need to do on the justice system. You need to standardize these metrics. I think you've got a great opportunity here, let's do it in Harris County. We would have a large part of the state finished if we standardized it in Harris County, and then we could model the rest of the state on that. We do have to make sure that it works in places like Hudspeth County; which has a lot fewer folks than you do and a lot of other issues. But I think we can do that. That's our kind of policy agenda this year is to get those performance metrics in place so that we can basically get things out of the way, because there are good folks in this mental health system. The MHMRA of Harris County, you have a tremendous number of wonderful people that are doing great programs everyday, but their hands are really tied by a lot of regulations, paperwork, requirements, that make it very difficult for them to do their job. We're trying to align around these metrics and we think if we did that, that would be really helpful.

I've told you I don't think the answer is more hospital beds. I'm not saying you may not need more access to hospitalization for certain groups. A lot of those new beds that are coming online are entirely targeted towards people with commercial insurance, not to say that no folks with commercial insurance go through the judicial system, they do. But the majority of folks that we are talking about and that are repeatedly going through are indigent, so what do we want to do? We're really good in Texas and in Harris County at crisis work. The CIRT, the NPC, all these cool acronyms are places that help people out, but we get hung up on keeping people in care.

The 1185 program is about keeping some of the most difficult people in care. A relatively small number, percentage-wise, but it's an important group and I think it's something that can be built on. If we had these performance metrics in place, so that we look at the responsiveness of the behavioral health system, we could see how well we respond in all cases, and how well we keep them in care. How do we keep them in care, and how do we get some of the regulations out that tie the hands of your MHMRA and give them service packages that they have to fit someone exactly in when the reality is that people don't always fit in the nice little boxes. You have to give clinicians a little bit of flexibility around this stuff.

This is where we're putting a lot of our effort in terms of system development, in how to build that capacity so that we don't overuse this wonderful crisis system that we've developed. We'd love to answer more questions when we have discussion. It is very exciting to be part of this and the Meadows Institute is very committed to helping out in this area. Tom Luce asked me what the priorities were for the year and I said that there was an effort going on in Harris County around diversion. But, after all, it's Harris County, which is really big and really hard, and quantity is a quality all of its own, and it is harder to do things when they're really big. But Tom told me about his education days, when he was a big education reformer. He told the cheerleaders and football players across Texas that they had to have passing grades if they were going to show up Friday night to the football game, and even more importantly, he took on their parents and somehow lived through that. He feels like we can do anything. We're here for the long term and we're excited about the opportunities here in Harris County.

Q&A and Discussion

QUESTION: I'm very frustrated. I do misdemeanor cases, and there are a lot of revolving door mentally ill misdemeanor cases, but probation departments are funded by the state and people that are accused of misdemeanors are often not as likely to take probation because they can get a short sentence. I'm interested in whether the assessments that you're doing in Harris County are being done for the misdemeanor courts. We do them in Travis County, but it's really only for the felony courts. Are you doing anything for the misdemeanor courts? Because I don't have that.

DR. TERESA MAY: Well, that's a great question. We actually just started our first misdemeanor pilot court this week. I didn't get into a lot of detail earlier because I didn't want to get way off of topic, but we are trying to speed up the process of assessment, both for felony and higher risk misdemeanors. The longer it takes for use to get these people assessed and get them engaged in the appropriate treatment and supervision, the more likely they're going to fail. It's a no-brainer. They are using drugs, shooting up, and mentally ill when they are arrested, and then we just put them on probation. If it takes me three months or four months to get all those assessments done, they're through the system and cycling back in again. I want to put a stop to that. I've done that before and, you know, there is a lot of challenges to it. In my previous life I did that only on felonies. What we did is we moved the assessment process before sentencing, so the assessment is either pre-plea, pre-sentence or it's post-plea, pre-sentence. What we do is if probation's on the table, it doesn't have to be agreed at that point – but it has to be on the table. The court resets the case for thirty days. The person may be out on bond. Then, probation is on the table – and I'm speaking about felony, we'll come around to misdemeanor – probation doesn't have to be agreed upon, but it has to be on the table. Then the court resets the case for thirty days. That person may be out on bond.

What's happening right now with our first three pilot courts is that there are individuals that are getting a PR bond to get out and as a condition of bond they get their assessment done. The process is designed to do the risk assessment first. If they are low risk then we don't spend very long identifying mental health. If they're medium or high risk, we're going to do more extensive screening for mental health and substance abuse and we're going to do it right then. It is one stop, but the more times you bring somebody back into a building or go get something done, the less likely they're going to show up, so when they get probation we already know what needs to happen. We know if they need to go to residential, we know if they need to be engaged in outpatient treatment, I know if they have a co-occurring problem and I need to get them in my dual diagnosis facility. I'm on top of that case. When we implemented this program before, we saw a 59 percent reduction in revocations, simply because we were moving fast and we were on top of these cases. If you don't move, these people are not going to get any better, so we stopped a lot of people coming back in the jail, which is really important.

Now to your question. I did not do that with misdemeanor in my prior life. It is an extreme challenge just because of the volume. However, there are high-risk misdemeanor cases. There are a lot of folks that just happen to be arrested on a misdemeanor this time. There are a lot of second DWIs in Harris County, and when I'm looking at these individuals, they have mental health issues, some of them are mixing drugs with the alcohol, it's a pretty scary situation. I'm working with my misdemeanor courts here. In misdemeanor, if they are put on probation, they are much more likely to show up if the judge says go get your assessment next door. What we're doing with misdemeanor, as soon as they're placed on probation, they walk straight over and go through the same process that felony is going through. Now here's the cool thing about Texas and I'm sorry if you all aren't from there, I have to brag on Texas a little bit. The risk assessment that we have just developed is a misdemeanor specific version of the tool. It measures the same critical factors, but it is focused on misdemeanor offenses, and it is highly predictive for misdemeanors, it works very well. What that does is that helps me be very efficient in getting them screened and assessed on the misdemeanor end. That's really important. My misdemeanor courts, just like my felony courts, have been really anxious to get involved in the new process and we just started our first misdemeanor court with Judge Brown this week. Ed Wells is back there, the court manager who has worked very hard with me. We'll be bringing more misdemeanor courts on as we go. You only have a short amount of time with misdemeanor, so the quicker I can intervene and get on top of those cases, the better it is. We do have limited funding, you're right, but we're getting smarter, and we're working through it. Carey Welebob is looking at me right now, she works hard with us. She gets phone calls from me when we need to do things, we're getting as creative as we can. That's the short answer, believe it or not.

QUESTION: Captain Bainbridge, your chief talked a little bit about the great resources that are available at the neuropsychiatric center for our CIRT teams to be able to do those drop offs. However, the capacity issue there is a deterrent on being able to fully utilize the system. I know Dr. Keller talked about how it isn't necessarily an overall bed capacity issue, but in those emergency situations that law enforcement are routinely involved with, hence the mental health division at HPD, is capacity an issue to be able to do those emergency detention orders and to be able to better facilitate the absence of incarceration on more of a clinical setting? It seems like added capacity to that system, which isn't necessarily a law enforcement issue but is more of a clinical one, it would certainly be very cost efficient.

CAPTAIN WENDY BAINBRIDGE: Thank you very much for the question, because I'd like to clean it up a bit. What we mean by needing more bed space is that it'd be nice to have step down care, long-term care that's affordable to keep people out of crisis mode. Last year we had seven thousand emergency detention orders from those thirty thousand calls for service that Chief Dirden was speaking about. Daily. NPC is on diversion. We have trained half our law enforcement officers on CIT, Crisis Intervention Training and learning how to handle those type of scenes, but it's had the unintended consequence of hitting capacity and it has highlighted the lack of bed space and care. As a result of that, people are just released and not really taken care of long term. They're not given the tools that they need, so they back up on the 911 system and get a police officer at their door instead of a mental health professional. Yes, absolutely, we need long-term care. We do. We need step down care, but the immediate need of crisis intervention training and having more facilities such as NPC instead of the area ERs of the Harris County jail is absolutely needed.

DR. ANDY KELLER: I would just fully agree with that. It's the flow through. I don't know numbers, available or needed, but it is a question, as well as whom you are using those beds for. New hospital beds are being built, but are they being aligned in the way NPC is?

That is a great front-end piece, but the next step is to untie the hands of your local mental health authority. They have a lot of restrictions on the about the type of practices and the number of hours that they can use. Then when they try to go out and recruit additional providers to be in their network they have problems. The requirements that the state put in place are a huge disincentive. They aren't going to be paid very much, and then they see the paper work and they just won't agree to it. It's both getting the right incentives and untying people's hands and then trusting our local clinicians and our local systems to come together. I have to say that's probably something that we also need to work on.

You've got great groups here like Clarissa's and it's been recommended that they be better represented in that process and to be there at the table. Often the mental health system are not great partners on this because we have a lot of barrier that prevent folks that you are concerned about from entering, and sometimes we make it harder than it needs to be. We need to work on that. But I think that being at the table and collaborating is something that we have to be a part of or we won't figure this stuff out.

MARC LEVIN: I want to ask about the role of civil commitment, including traditional civil commitment to a residential facility and the potential use of civil outpatient commitment. Sometimes we hear that someone is charged or arrested for some really minor things like criminal trespass. Part of the goal in prosecuting them is to get them treatment, but maybe we'd be better of strengthening the civil, including civil outpatient commitment, as an alternative to criminal prosecution.

DR. TERESA MAY: Now, Marc, you're assuming everybody wants treatment. Right? So you're talking civil commitment, which is not that easy to do and I don't know if Wendy wants to talk about that or not? You guys looking into that?

CAPTAIN WENDY BAINBRIDGE: No. When I mentioned seven thousand emergency detention orders last year, 24% had a criminal nexus to them, but only one percent of those thirty thousand calls ended in an arrest. Already, CIT training is the largest practiced use of diversion. We have an emergency detention order that the state of Texas has allowed peace officers to have and that is just a one-page form for an evaluation. We don't do many civil commitments beyond that. Of the seven thousand emergency detention orders we had last year, eighty percent doctors wanted to keep, but only twenty percent of that eighty wen on to get committed. That is the process after law enforcement has handed them off at NPC or an area ER. We don't really have a lot going on regarding civil commitments beyond the EDO.

DR. TERESA MAY: I'm not the best person to talk about this, so if there's someone in the room that has more expertise, I'm happy for you to sit up and talk. I have worked with individuals in the county jail where we have someone that's just very, very sick. Maybe not to the point of incompetency, but they're probably pretty close. We have them in the jail, we have them outside of the jail, reporting to probation. I have families calling me, how can I get my family member in the hospital? There are a lot of challenges to the civil commitment process. They don't stay long, and they're usually right back. I know in the jail one of the other issues is – and also even among offenders on probation - is refusing medications. A lot of the folks that are getting arrested and reporting to us are refusing to take their medications. That is probably one of the biggest challenges and barriers that anyone has. Including our mental health partners. There are limitations, even in jail. If somebody refuses their meds, you can't automatically force medications. There are a very limited number of ways you can actually even get an order to force medications. Then the question is how long they keep them, what happens, and does it answer things in the long run? My other point is that if they're low risk, absolutely, I wish we could look at that more, if they don't have a lot of those other criminogenic risk factors. If they're not, you know, we definitely need access to get the psychiatric symptoms addressed, but we have to address the drug problems, the criminogenic risk problems, or this will never stop. That's what everyone needs to understand.

JERRY MADDEN: That leads to one of the things that I was going to mention up here, which is how important coordination is. If you don't have that then each group and agency is only going to do what is best for their budget instead of the system as a whole. We've seen that many times out there. If you can coordinate it in such a manner so that the ultimate goal is the best results that you can possibly get for the overall system, and coordinate that funding, you will in fact see a reduced cost and at the same time a better result.

DR. ANDY KELLER: Marc, I also think that the fundamental coordination and collaboration among is a more important factor. I think the outpatient commitment is one tool, but there are other tools around motivational interviewing, and frankly the motivation of your treatment system to want to keep people in care. You're working at cross-purposes versus working together, and a lot of times, we want to make individuals collaborate, and there's a limit to that. To keep people in care ongoing really requires a motivational framework and requires partners willing to work together.

What I would say is that we're trying to really emphasize at the Institute that the mechanisms whereby local control can be coordinated and then implemented. By that, we mean people who often are not on the same page, because there's a lot of struggles around everybody trying to live their mission out locally, to get them to align around some common goals and then if they come up with outpatient commitment or something they want to do, then great. It's more important the local driven aspect, to me, and the coordination than the specific tool.

DR. TERESA MAY: Well, and let me piggyback on something, Marc. And I think this is important as we're going into session, to look at what we've historically done in criminal justice. I have a lot of mentally ill offenders on probation that need intervention. We're working with them. We start to see them melt down, get off their meds, get symptomatic, and we know the wheels are coming off. Getting them an appointment real quick is not an easy thing. There are other times when - if I could get them in a crisis bed - we would have a shot at stabilizing them. They're willing, they just – they don't have the skills to do it. There really is a need to mesh these systems together, but there's not a mechanism to do that. My mechanism is not easy at all, so we end up trying to work with a system that can't respond. Something else that's important to understand is that the criminal justice and the mental health system has kind of been meshed together because of the circumstances. There's a really big need for it, but our mental health system worries a lot. They don't really like the criminal justice folks showing up all the time. They're not necessarily comfortable with everything that we do and there's an education process and possibly, as Andy has said, we really need to look at the system design as to how we can work and communicate better with the criminal justice and mental health system in getting people services at the right time and preventing an arrest or preventing people from having to go to jail.

JERRY MADDEN: That gets into the statement I made earlier about the financing and the organizing, and it's important to know where those points are at, whether it be at your local city council, whether it be at your county commissioner's court where that coordination can be done, whether that's at the state of Texas in what we do or whether it's someplace else and we need to put some other pressures on additional groups.

RYAN SULLIVAN, *Policy Advisor, Harris County Sheriff's Office*: Dr. Keller, I appreciate everything that you said because you've hit on every one of the policy prerogatives that we've been addressing and dealing with on a daily basis. With regard to capacity, we have grave concern for capacity for diversion, but we're also concerned with capacity post-release. Right now, we have a big problem with providing the continuity of care after people have left our facility. The one barrier that I wanted to ask you if you could talk about is our state limitations to funding the big three diagnoses. Right now, the state only funds MHMRA to provide for schizophrenia, bipolar disorder, and major depression. Inside the jail, we're giving comprehensive coverage for PTSD, anxiety disorder, but naturally that treatment's for naught when they're released back into the community.

DR. ANDY KELLER: That's a really important question and it's particularly important for some particular subgroups, like veterans, for example. Post-traumatic stress is not on that list and that's a big barrier. A little known fact though, is that the last legislative session saw that barrier removed. There is no real restriction around the big three diagnoses. What there is, is there's a traditional funding stream that was designed around the big three diagnoses that was not increased in a way that people sort of perceive as large enough to handle more, so it's at the discretion of local jurisdictions about how much they want to stray from those. It requires a little bit of it is getting out of the mindset and that's why we think it's really the local system coming together and making decisions around that. You have a hundred and ten million dollars a year more being spent here through your district projects. Did you prioritize any of the district projects around the things we're talking about today? And if not, why? I mean, those are questions that I think can only be answered here in Harris County and I'm not saying that those other needs that the district projects are addressing aren't important, I'm not saying some of them aren't addressing this population. But I think that you basically have to make the local decision about how to do that and then you have to operationalize it.

Some of it gets down to two similar protocols, like something Dr. May and I have been talking about. ANSA is a protocol that the mental health system needs to use. If there was a way to get ANSA more used – I mean, she's doing very comprehensive assessments. It'll take about ten more minutes at the end of her assessment to put it into an ANSA format and if we had that in there in a reliable way, that makes a very nice pipeline to get folks over into the mental health system to help inform and make decisions about that. That's a very functionally driven tool that looks at level of functioning. It's less about diagnosis. The other thing I'll tell you, too, is I wouldn't make too big of an issue about this, the big three thing. It's an issue, but we have to keep it in perspective because, we're doing a study right now of all the adults in the Medicaid system with serious mental illness and the difference in the number between the big three who have big needs and the others is, I mean, PTS involves subgroups, but once you get beyond that, it's not that many folks. Most people figure out how to give somebody a qualified diagnosis, so I mean, it's really moving to more functioning and local decisions around how to implement that.

KATHY GRIFFIN, *Policy Advisor, Harris County Sheriff's Office*: I just wanted to ask about, being a person myself in recovery, and dealing with so many individuals in the Harris County jail that have mental health issues along with substance abuse and dual diagnosis, a lot of them that are attending my classes and my groups are so heavily medicated they can't stay awake to program. Is there anybody doing any research in psychotropics that are not addictive and not so drowsy, with a drowsy effect? Because it is so hard to work with individuals and work on rehabilitating them and they're not coherent and they can't stay awake and alert. And a lot of them use the excuse that, well, they diagnosed me bipolar so I need a chick. And they focus on thinking that being bipolar, ADHD, or ADD is an excuse for me to not have to get a job. And our MHMRA people reeducating or educating for the first time when they're coherent enough that that's why you take the medicine, if you're depressed, you're under the blanket and couldn't come out, and now you're on the medication, why are you still under the blanket?

DR. TERESA MAY: Kathy, we recently reopened the dual diagnosis residential facility, and it's designed to deal with exactly the issues you're talking about. It's designed for this specific population that uses drugs and has serious mental health problems. What is absolutely critical, and several people have hit the nail on the head today, is that we are in a position to provide valuable information to the psychiatrists when we need some medication adjustment, because of these kinds of difficulties. When they're sitting in jail it's a little bit different, so you need to keep that in mind, but the most effective programs for mentally ill criminal justice involved individuals, involve collaboration between the criminal justice partner and the mental health professional. That is a free flowing communication, quick acting and co-educating these individuals and working with them. It's an everyday thing. My hope is that we get to a point in Harris County where we're doing even – we're going to continue to improve that, and break down the barriers.

ANDY KELLER: The only thing I would add is I think we also need to set the goal that – to not just have programs that do these things, but to have systems. That we have to have, basically every entry point in our system has to be co-occurring capable. It's ubiquitous. We have to be able to deal with that at every entry point in every treatment program and I think that there's great things to model on, but that should be our goal.

JERRY MADDEN: I want to thank everybody, particularly the panel, for a great job. I think it was very educational, very informative, thank you all. And now I believe we got about a ten-minute break, and then they're supposed to then be in for lunch. Don't miss the next speaker. He's my co-conspirator in a lot of stuff that we did in Texas, my friend John Whitmire.

Reforming Texas

INTRODUCTION: Judge Oscar Hale, Jr.
District Judge, the 406th District court in Laredo, Texas

I am truly honored and humbled to be here with you today. When I received an invitation from Marc and the Texas Foundation on Public Policy, I thought about it and asked myself, "Why are they considering me an expert in drug courts? I guess I've been doing it for five years and maybe that qualifies, but I certainly don't consider myself an expert." But I hope that some of the things that I have to share with you today will help you in providing services to your community like it has our community in Laredo. And certainly a little intimidating to say a few words here before the honorable Senator Whitmire, but I'll do my best.

I'm glad that I was here early enough also to hear some of the comments and remarks made by some of the other speakers. My jurisdiction is in Webb County. Laredo, Texas. It's a border town to the Republic of Mexico. It's – I guess we brag about it being the largest or busiest inland port for commercial trade. Unfortunately with that also comes one of the major corridors for drug trafficking in our country. What we see a lot in our community is that a lot of those drugs linger and so it ends up in our schools. I've been on the bench ten years and, as Marc mentioned, we started a program called Let's All Rise To The Challenge. We go to the school campuses, and I hold actual court sentencing there. We have three or four sentencing on drug cases and we invite our drug court participants to speak to the students. We go to the high schools and middle schools. What shocked me, I guess about four or five years ago, was that one of our elementary school teachers along with the principal called to invite me in to beg us to go to their school and hold a court session there. I said, well, elementary, they're a little too young, I can go as a speaker and address them, but I don't know if they'll get the concept of an actual court setting or proceeding. The response was, unfortunately, that in that campus, they had one nine year old, a third grader, arrested for dealing drugs on campus. Not in possession of drugs, dealing drugs on campus. Sheriff Garcia mentioned earlier that we need to address the demand – and he was talking about prostitution – but unfortunately, the prostitution victims are often addicted to drugs. I agree with the concept of addressing the demand. We need to address the demand early. That's why we're doing that in Laredo with our 'courts in school' program. We're trying to educate our youth about the dangers and consequences of drugs by seeing – by having them see firsthand the individuals that are sentenced and handcuffed and shackled walking out of their gymnasium or library, and listening to their testimonials.

Sometimes you have no idea what these defendants are going to say. I remember one defendant in particular wearing the classic black and white jumpsuit from the jail. He was twenty-one years old and I had just sentenced him to five years for possession of cocaine. He was telling the students there that he actually attended this school. We didn't set it up that way, it just worked out. He's telling them, I was in this campus a few years ago, this middle school campus. He said that when I sat there like you are, I didn't know what the consequences were. But he's handcuffed and shackled and he told them, here they are in black and white. I thought that was pretty deep. The students were being very attentive, and he mentioned to them that while he was in custody for seven months, his girlfriend had given birth to his daughter who was six months old and he said, I have not been able to hold my own daughter.

Now let me go talk a little bit more about my drug court or our drug court. We started our drug court in 2009. I was sharing with John earlier about how I became interested in mental health and drug courts. When I took the bench in 2005 one of my fellow district judges, the honorable Manuel Flores, was a little overwhelmed. We talked about whether we needed more judges and determined that it depends. We can probably all work a little harder, and get more things done, but in this case, he was overwhelmed. My docket was a small docket, so I went ahead and accepted a transfer of about four hundred cases, all felony drug cases. What I started seeing was the revolving door. We were sentencing people to county time and state jail time, and then seeing them right back. In some cases, there are individuals who ended up dying of drug overdoses, waiting for their adjudication.

I was fortunate enough to meet and be inspired by the retired judge John Creuzot. I think he is one of the most passionate judges and strongest proponents of drug courts. He inspired me, motivated me to come back to Laredo and start a drug court program, and today we have our sobriety treatment program. We address the alcohol dependent participants, and we just started our veterans treatment program a year ago. I can proudly say that our success rate is high, as far as reoffending goes among our graduates, only twenty-five percent have actually reoffended. The participants who are in our program we can monitor for drug use as well, not just reoffending. The drug use varies of course, but the reoffending, recidivism rate, is for the active participants – and sometimes they abscond, is under twenty percent. So, you know, drug court works. I guess that's what I'm here to say.

We started implementing our medication assistance treatment for our veterans treatment program with our vivitrol. I'm sure a lot of you know about the drug vivitrol, the injection form of naltrexone. What we found is that those individuals who have started using vivitrol and are participating in this program because of their mental health issues are more attentive at the individual sessions and group sessions, more receptive to treatment and as a result, employment rate has gone higher, there's less criminal activity committed by them and, as I mentioned, we just started our veterans treatment program and as of today none of our veterans have reoffended. We have thirty-five veterans in our program right now. Our veterans treatment program also has two licensed professional counselors who are also veterans. They have firsthand knowledge of the issues and I think that's worked very well for our program. I guess I'll leave with this note. I was asked also what I did before, what my aspirations were before becoming a lawyer, and I actually wanted to join the Drug Enforcement Administration, because my father and my uncle are all in law enforcement. My thoughts at the time were, before law school, I want to join the fight on the war on drugs. Again, I talked about my hometown and all the things that go on there. I saw that growing up. But what I've come to learn is that there's a better way to fight the war on drugs and that's by fighting one addiction at a time. Every day, in every way and in every place. I think if we all do our part we can win this war.

Sen. John Whitmire

Chairman, Texas Senate Committee on Corrections

I want to thank each of you for being here and the opportunity to speak to you. I can't think of a better summit topic than pretrial and mental health solutions. I'm going to walk you kind of through where we've been, where we are, and where we need to go. You've heard a lot today, you've heard from the practitioners that make such a difference, but if you don't remember anything else as participants, as you go back to your fields, remember that criminal justice is a system. I deal with all facets of the criminal justice system on a daily basis. I am the police officer spokesman in Austin. I have a great working relation with the district attorneys. I work with correction officers and administrators everyday, and I could go on. What we have to emphasize and learn and recognize is that what you do at this end impacts the corrections system. What the parole officer does will impact recidivism, which will then impact the prison population. How the district attorney decides to prosecute impacts the correction facilities. The conditions of probation will impact revocations, which then impact the corrections system. What each agency does as affects the entirety of the system, but we still have individuals, local sheriffs, local organizations and associations that say, "To hell with the rest of the system, my job is to arrest people. And I'm going to go after trace cocaine even if when they get to court there's not even enough to test."

Please, arresting officer and your union, my dear friends, recognize that that is only taking your officers off the street. It is only overcrowding your jail, and ultimately compounding our problems at our correction facilities. If you don't remember anything else, leave here recognizing that we're all in this together, from the earliest arrest. In fact, that is true even from the school systems and how we deal with school discipline. The reentry system that we barely have certainly impacts whether parolees are successful. So we're in a system, and I want to emphasize that, but then let's quickly drill down on where we've been, where we are, and where we need to go.

The first time that I went to the House in 1973 was as a young state representative. Then, the prison system was a very small rural system. 1981 was the first time that I ever really heard about the issue of overcrowding in prisons. Bill Clements, the first Republican in a hundred and fifty years, vetoed the addition of ten thousand prison beds in 1981. He didn't think that we needed to spend that money, so he was obviously a businessman. That veto got our attention, we did pretty well in the 80s. Then, by 1983, our criminal justice system was completely broken just like most in the nation. Crack cocaine drove that overpopulation, and we weren't prepared for it. In '93, I had been in the Senate for ten years and was chairing intergovernmental affairs. But our chairman of criminal justice, Ted Lyons was lost and Bob Bullock, a very tough lieutenant governor, called me into his office and said, "I want you to chair criminal justice." And I said, "No, no, no, no." I thought that the fix was to end my career that session.

The criminal justice system was a revolving door then. Offenders were serving one month for every year that they were sentenced. Life sentences were less than ten years, it was totally dysfunctional. There was no classification, no distinguishing between violent and non-violent offenders. A rapist would be let out to put in a car thief. There were sixty thousand inmates in the prison system with thirty thousand backed up in the county jails because there was nowhere to place them. Many were paroled without leaving the county jail. It was a total mess and I didn't want to do it. I'd never even been on that committee, and I wasn't a criminal attorney.

But after thinking it over I came back and said, "Let's go!" You don't tell your boss no, or you won't get another chance. I recognized my limitations and surrounded myself with people like Tony Fabelo, Lawrence Coleman, crime victim advocates, and prosecutors. The penal code had been sunsetted the year before and we had to rewrite it. It came out as one of the toughest penal codes in the nation. You don't have to wait for three strikes in Texas, you commit a violent offense then we know what to do. We started classifications to be more efficient. That was where we came up with the idea of state jails. These were heavy on treatment.

But then Governor Bush came around. We had instituted a lot of treatment as a part of the state jail concept, but Governor Bush said, "Hey, what's the issue here? I quit drinking on my own." He had a tough wife that read him the riot act. After an all-nighter she said (it is in his book), "Either quit drinking, or you and I are going to have serious problems." So Governor George W. Bush quit drinking on his own. Unfortunately, you and I know that that model won't work for many people. They don't have support systems, resources, or families. But we had to cut back in our treatment, and by 2003 there wasn't much left.

In 2005 Jerry Madden came around. We had met in Chicago at a conference, and I sat next to him. He was an engineer that was of my opinion and a good solid Republican. He became the chair of criminal justice in the House and we began meeting and talking. He was analytical, smart, and had a conscience. Many people have asked me how I got so much treatment passed through in '07 after having been talking about it for thirteen years. I tell them that first of all, I got Jerry Madden as a partner in the House to talk the talk there. And number two I said it enough times. You say something enough times and finally they start to believe it. I said again and again that there is a better model than locking up everyone that comes before a judge.

Judge Gist from Beaumont, who is on the TDCJ board, taught me in the 90s that the easiest thing a judge can do is send someone to prison. It clears the docket and you don't see them again. He told me that it takes work to keep someone out of prison. I learned a great deal from Judge Gist. In 2007 we had a backlog again, we were out of prison space. I sit on the finance committee, just to the left of Steve Ogden, who didn't understand the need for treatment. He was always confusing parole and probation when we were funding. He would mix them up. He is a Naval Academy graduate, a nuclear physicist, a submarine commander, and one day after a committee hearing I said, "Steve, you have got to learn the difference between probation and parole." He said, "Whitmire, you're not going to get your funding calling me stupid." I said, "Well, learn the damned difference." Dewhurst and the leadership wanted three new prisons. I spoke in finance and tried to explain that we couldn't operate the ones that we have, that we were three thousand correction officers short.

Trust me, treatment works; I've seen it. Instead of those three new prisons we got six thousand treatment beds. Ogden would still say publicly that it was

Whitmire's "hug-a-thug" program, but there is nothing soft on crime about getting someone off drugs, making them get their life together, support their family and become a taxpayer. That's often harder than incarceration. If he wanted to call it my "hug-a-thug" program that was fine, because it works. We created several thousand beds at the front end. As a condition of probation you would go to a central unit, like Sugar Land. You would spend six months in counseling and treatment, and recidivism rates lowered in those populations. We put additional beds inside the prisons and that worked as well.

Another one that is really working is intermediate sanction facilities. If parolees have a bad day and they don't show up or have another minor infraction, they no longer get immediately send to prison. Unless they commit a new crime they aren't going back. But if they don't follow our rules, we have intermediate sanctions. These are working well and are lowering recidivism.

Another thing that I am very proud about is the way we handle DWI offenders now. Everyone knows that drinking and driving can kill just like a gun, but when that same individual isn't drinking, no one is in danger. We've spoken about the difference between the people that we are afraid of and those we are angry at several times today. We need to incarcerate those that we are afraid of, child molesters, rapists, murderers. Those I have no sympathy with. We can lock them up for serious time. But to have the resources for that, you can't waste them on the people that you are simply angry with. People convicted of DWIs, when they aren't drinking, we aren't afraid of them.

Most of these people are alcoholics. You don't go to prison until after your third conviction. Most people can make a mistake on their first conviction and then get their life together and learn not to drink and drive. After the third conviction, it is obvious that they have a serious problem. This morning we have about fifty-five hundred people incarcerated across the state for their third or more DWI. In 2007 they would have gone through without treatment. Now we have created a location in Henderson that deals with this. This morning we have five hundred DWI offenders who are learning to cope with their drinking issue. And it's working well. To TDCJ's credit they want another facility like that.

We need to focus on the treatment. Even just last year, Mothers Against Drunk Drivers were asking for more and more punishment instead of treatment. We need to talk about fixing people's problems. Last year, we released four thousand people from TDCJ who have been sent there for their DWI convictions and they didn't receive a day of treatment in our prisons. That is unconscionable. That in itself ought to be against the law. How do you lock someone up for drinking and driving and then let them out years later without any treatment? We have to work on this.

When I worked with Jerry in 2007, Texas became a model for the nation. Marc Levin and the Texas Public Policy Foundation became our partner. It was great to have such credibility. But now we find ourselves in 2014 with a lot of unfinished business. We are still incarcerating too many people. At the Harris County jail there is probably anywhere from a thousand to fifteen hundred misdemeanor offenders that haven't been to court yet, in jail because they can't afford the bond. In Dallas or San Antonio they could do a PR bond if they met the criteria for non-flight risk. The lack of this is overcrowding the Harris County jail, and these people are losing their jobs if they can't go in to work. These people aren't a danger to society, they just make us mad.

A few years ago they made prostitution a felony. Highland Park was the lead sponsor and John Cornyn carried it because Highland Park didn't want prostitutes on their street corners. But these people are not who I'm afraid of. I don't like their lifestyle, but this morning we probably have a little over three hundred prostitutes locked up in our maximum-security prison for women in Gatesville. Dallas has a successful prostitution court, Corpus has a good one, and I carried a bill that required counties with populations over two hundred and fifty thousand to create a prostitution court. This is because as we've learned from drug courts, DWI courts, mental health courts, and now military courts, specialty courts work, if the judge and counselors see the same groups and learn what resources to use.

We can't continue to waste prison space. I appeal to my fiscal conservative Republicans – if you don't do it because it is the human thing to do, do it to save money. It is important to keep these ladies in diversion programs. I have spoken to Kathy Griffin's clientele, gone and heard her work and counseling, and it has shown me the importance of these programs and reentry support. That is what I was speaking about earlier. We are a system. Policy officers, judges, DAs, you have to understand how you affect these women at the front end. If we don't improve then I have to increase prison space, which I'm opposed to. Let's keep them in the community, then you can have a successful reentry program.

Prostitution is just one component though. We've got twelve thousand women locked up in Gatesville this morning, and nearly every one of them are non-violent. There may be a few violent women that have done some dangerous things, but most are non-violent, in for drug or alcohol abuse. Most of these women are not a threat to society. When they go to prison, they might not be the most law-abiding citizens, but most of them are good mothers. When you lock up a man in prison, it has a profound impact. But oftentimes the women we lock up were the sole provider for their family. Most of those women respond to treatment, whether it be in the mental health court, a DWI court, or the prostitution court. Do you know how many babies we had born in prison last year? A hundred and ninety-eight babies were born in prison last year. These women were pregnant when they came through the system. Some judges actually have told me, "Yeah, I sent her to prison, because that's the only place she's going to get any prenatal care." Now I appreciate your thought, judge, but I would much rather put her in a diversion program and keep her in the community.

Another thing that I'm very proud of is the BAMBI program, the Baby and Mother Bonding Initiative. A few years ago, in the mid-90s, I was at a female prison, speaking with one of the inmates. This lady wouldn't make eye contact with me, and cried the entire time. I asked her if I could held, and told her that I wanted to learn from her. She said, "I'm crying because they took my baby away from me two weeks ago." I was so new to the committee at the time I had to ask, "What do you mean they took your baby away?" She was in for her fifth DWI. She shouldn't have been in prison in the first place, but she is from a little area, with no resources, but that situation should have been handled differently. She could have been restricted to her house. She is obviously a very serious alcoholic, but she was pregnant when she went to prison. In

League City they have facilities for pregnant women, where they go about six weeks before their due date. But then they would wait just about until the time that a woman went into labor to head for the prison hospital. In those days, and still in some cases, you would have the baby one day and they would take it the next. The child would either be placed in adoption or left with your family. I was committed from that conversation on to doing better.

There are other areas that we could do better in as well. We really have to work on prison officials on a regular basis. In northeast Houston, they have twenty mothers this morning. Most of these women are only in there for a couple of years, but that may be too long to have the child wait. The good news is those twenty mothers. Texas Department of Criminal Justice confines in a confined apartment that now get to keep and bond with their baby.

I'd like to close with the subject of criminalized school behavior. There is no question that they over ticket and over police the youth and parents for truancy. Last session with Royce West we significantly reduced the number of ticketings for things like being out of your seat, throwing an eraser, cursing, all of those things could have been ticketed before. Now you have a complainant, a teacher or administrator and it has to be for a violation of the penal code. That significantly reduces the ticketing. But we still ticket for truancy, and there is no reason that giving a five hundred dollar ticket to the student and/or parent solves the root cause of the truancy.

I have documented a case where an undocumented mother with an eight year-old asked me for help when she got a ticket because he didn't attend school that week. No one went out to see that her car had died, that she had no family, no one to ask for help. Our school administrators need to learn what it is like to like to live in the real world. They have to be sensitive to situations. For example, an inner city student, fourteen years old, wasn't attending school and got ticket. When the court system sent a manager to her home they found out that she was pregnant and had no maternity clothes. She couldn't go to school because she was embarrassed. Why would school administrators or legislators want that to be a criminal justice issue?

We worked on expulsions and suspension last year and we are going to address them again. There is no question that too many students are being suspended or expelled. After studying at the national level, we have documented that nothing good comes from out-of-school suspensions. There are very rare exceptions, but usually, when you send a child home in the middle of the day, without supervision they connect with gangs and troublemakers.

Let me impress upon you another aspect of this: there is over-representation of the African American community in school suspensions. In 2012, eighty-four percent of our African American males in Texas public schools were suspended one or more times. That is nearly everyone. Some of these were suspended more than eleven times. Why did the school not learn after one, two, or three suspensions that it wasn't working? Once they are entered into the system this way these kids get a case number. You can go to TJJD, the Texas youth facilities, and talk to the young people there. Nearly every one of them, every one of them, was suspended and had a bad experience in their school career, and many dropped out. So to our school officials, to the criminal justice system, we must do better starting at the school setting, because that's when we can detect the problems at a very early stage.

Before I conclude, I'd like to emphasize mental health. The criminal justice system has become the mental health service provider for the state of Texas. The Harris County jail probably treats more mental health patients than anywhere in state or county government. TDCJ's current population is a hundred and fifty thousand people, in a hundred and eight locations. We've actually shut down three prisons in the last four years, because we've tried treatment our population has begun dropping. But the current number is still huge. We documented that thirty-two thousand inmates last spring had been in a community mental health program before they committed their current crimes. They were getting counseling and treatment, but because of budget cuts in 2003 we no longer have those resources so those people were released.

Then they have a bad day. They are schizophrenic, or bipolar, and they go home and assault a family member or a neighbor. Law enforcement is summoned, then they assault the police officer and welcome to the criminal justice system. We have to convince lawmakers that if you spend money on mental health at the front end, we will get a long ways toward addressing overcrowding, prison conditions, and cost. Our problem is much larger if you consider the people that have never been diagnosed, or those that are put in administrative segregation. They still overuse that mechanism at nearly every prison.

I'll close now. And please remember that we are all in this together and every step and every component has a downstream or upstream impact. I had a conversation with Dan Patrick yesterday because some law enforcement groups want to make the first time burglary of a vehicle a felony. I understand that that is frustrating, my car has been broken into, and it makes you angry. But I have to worry about prioritizing jail and prison space.

In conclusion, I want to lock up the people that I'm afraid of; I don't want to mess with the ones that I'm mad at. Someone told me, "Whitmire, you should have copyrighted the phrase 'smart on crime' back in 1993." Because everyone in the legislature is already tough on crime. We don't want to be held up. I've begged for my life when I was robbed at gunpoint. I don't want anyone else to go through that experience. The man that robbed me spent twelve years in Abilene prison, and I believe is doing well outside of prison. The bottom line is that we have to continue to be smart. It saves money, it saves lives, and we can do a lot better.

About Right on Crime

Right on Crime is a national campaign to promote successful, conservative solutions on American criminal justice policy—reforming the system to ensure public safety, shrink government, and save taxpayers money. By sharing research and policy ideas and mobilizing strong conservative voices, we work to raise awareness of the growing support for effective reforms within the conservative movement. We are transforming the debate on criminal justice in America.

Our Statement Of Principles

As members of the nation's conservative movement, we strongly support constitutionally limited government, transparency, individual liberty, personal responsibility, and free enterprise. We believe public safety is a core responsibility of government because the establishment of a well- functioning criminal justice system enforces order and respect for every person's right to property and life, and ensures that liberty does not lead to license.

Conservatives correctly insist that government services be evaluated on whether they produce the best possible results at the lowest possible cost, but too often this lens of accountability has not focused as much on public safety policies as other areas of government. As such, corrections spending has expanded to become the second fastest growing area of state budgets—trailing only Medicaid.

Conservatives are known for being tough on crime, but we must also be tough on criminal justice spending. That means demanding more cost-effective approaches that enhance public safety. A clear example is our reliance on prisons, which serve a critical role by incapacitating dangerous offenders and career criminals but are not the solution for every type of offender. And in some instances, they have the unintended consequence of hardening nonviolent, low-risk offenders—making them a greater risk to the public than when they entered.

Applying the following conservative principles to criminal justice policy is vital to achieving a cost-effective system that protects citizens, restores victims, and reforms wrongdoers.

1. As with any government program, the criminal justice system must be transparent and include performance measures that hold it account- able for its results in protecting the public, lowering crime rates, reducing re-offending, collecting victim restitution and conserving taxpayers' money.

2. Crime victims, along with the public and taxpayers, are among the key "consumers" of the criminal justice system; the victim's conception of justice, public safety, and the offender's risk for future criminal conduct should be prioritized when determining an appropriate punishment.

3. The corrections system should emphasize public safety, personal responsibility, work, restitution, community service, and treatment— both in probation and parole, which supervise most offenders, and in prisons.

4. An ideal criminal justice system works to reform amenable offenders who will return to society through harnessing the power of families, charities, faith-based groups, and communities.

5. Because incentives affect human behavior, policies for both offenders and the corrections system must align incentives with our goals of public safety, victim restitution and satisfaction, and cost-effectiveness, thereby moving from a system that grows when it fails to one that rewards results.

6. Criminal law should be reserved for conduct that is either blameworthy or threatens public safety, not wielded to grow government and undermine economic freedom.

These principles are grounded in time-tested conservative truths— constitutionally limited government, transparency, individual liberty, personal responsibility, free enterprise, and the centrality of the family and community. All of these are critical to addressing today's criminal justice challenges. It is time to apply these principles to the task of delivering a better return on taxpayers' investments in public safety. Our security, prosperity, and freedom depend on it.

Right on Crime Signatories

Newt Gingrich
Former Speaker of the House of Representatives

Grover Norquist
Americans for Tax Reform

Gov. Rick Perry
Former Governor of Texas

Gov. Asa Hutchinson
Governor of Arkansas

Chuck Colson (1931-2012)
Prison Fellowship Ministries

William J. Bennett
Former Secretary of Education and
Federal "Drug Czar"

Jeb Bush
Former Governor of Florida

Ken Cuccinelli
Former Attorney General, Virginia

David Keene
Former Chairman, American Conservative Union
and National Rifle Association

J.C. Watts
Former Member of the U.S. House of
Representatives, Oklahoma's 4th District

Edwin Meese III
Former U.S. Attorney General

Stephen Moore
The Heritage Foundation

Pat Nolan
Director, Criminal Justice Reform Project,
American Conservative Union Foundation

Richard Viguerie
ConservativeHQ.com

Brooke Rollins
Texas Public Policy Foundation

Ken Blackwell
Former Ohio Secretary of State

Ralph Reed
Founder, Faith and Freedom Coalition

Eli Lehrer
R Street Institute

Rebecca Hagelin
Executive Committee, Council for National
Policy

Tony Perkins
Family Research Council

B. Wayne Hughes, Jr.
Businessman and Philanthropist

Henry Juszkiewicz
CEO of Gibson Guitar

Penny Nance
Concerned Women for America

John J. DiLulio, Jr.
University of Pennsylvania

Ward Connerly
American Civil Rights Institute

George Kelling
Manhattan Institute

Gary Bauer
American Values

David Barton
WallBuilders

Rabbi Daniel Lapin
American Alliance of Jews and Christians

Michael Reagan
The Reagan Legacy Foundation

Monica Crowley, Ph.D.
Fox News political analyst

Erick Erickson
Founder of RedState.com

Alfred Regnery
Law Enforcement Legal Defense Fund

For a more complete list of Right on Crime signatories—including state-based signatories and partners—see rightoncrime.com

The Conservative Case for Criminal Justice Reform

PUBLIC SAFETY. Because government exists to secure liberties that can only be enjoyed to the extent there is public safety, state and local policymakers must make fighting crime their top priority, including utilizing prisons to incapacitate violent offenders and career criminals. Prisons are overused, however, when nonviolent offenders who may be safely supervised in the community are given lengthy sentences. Prisons provide diminishing returns when such offenders emerge more disposed to re-offend than when they entered prison.

RIGHT-SIZING GOVERNMENT. Nearly 1 in every 100 American adults is in prison or jail. When you add in those on probation or parole, almost 1 in 33 adults is under some type of control by the criminal justice system. When Ronald Reagan was president, the total correctional control rate was 1 in every 77 adults. This represents a significant expansion of government power. By reducing excessive sentence lengths and holding nonviolent offenders accountable through prison alternatives, public safety can often be achieved consistent with a legitimate, but more limited, role for government.

FISCAL DISCIPLINE. The prison system now costs states more than $50 billion per year, up from $11 billion in the mid-1980s. It has been the second-fastest growing area of state budgets, trailing only Medicaid, and consumes one in every 14 general fund dollars. Conservatives must address runaway spending on prisons just as they do with education and health care, subjecting the same level of skepticism and scrutiny to all expenditures of taxpayers' funds.

VICTIM SUPPORT. In 2008, Texas probationers paid $45 million in restitution to victims, but prisoners paid less than $500,000 in restitution, fines, and fees. Making victims whole must be prioritized when determining appropriate punishments for offenders. The criminal justice system should be structured to ensure that victims are treated with dignity and respect and that they may participate in the criminal justice process and receive restitution.

PERSONAL RESPONSIBILITY. With some 5 million offenders on probation or parole, it's critical that the corrections system hold these offenders accountable for their actions by holding a job or performing community service, attending required treatment programs, and staying crime- and drug-free. When the system has real teeth, the results can be dramatic: offenders subject to swift, certain and commensurate sanctions for rule violations in Hawaii's HOPE program are less than half as likely to be arrested or fail a drug test.

GOVERNMENT ACCOUNTABILITY. More than 40 percent of released offenders return to prison within three years of release, and in some states, recidivism rates are closer to 60 percent. As Right on Crime signatories Newt Gingrich and Mark Earley have asked, "[i]f two-thirds of public school students dropped out, or two-thirds of all bridges built collapsed within three years, would citizens tolerate it?" Corrections funding should be partly linked to outcomes and should implement proven strategies along the spectrum between basic probation and prison.

FAMILY PRESERVATION. According to National Review, "40 percent of low-income men who father a child out of wedlock have already been in jail or prison by the time their first son or daughter is born." The family unit is the foundation of society. In a society in which too many young men are incarcerated, marriage rates are depressed and far too many children grow up in single-parent homes. Instead of harming families, the corrections system must harness the power of charities, faith-based groups, and communities to reform offenders and preserve families.

FREE ENTERPRISE. The Constitution lists only three federal crimes, but the number of statutory federal crimes has now swelled to around 4,500. This is to say nothing of the thousands of bizarre state-level crimes, such as the 11 felonies in Texas related to the harvesting of oysters. The explosion of non-traditional criminal laws grows government and undermines economic freedom. Criminal law should be reserved for conduct that is blameworthy or threatens public safety, not wielded to regulate non-fraudulent economic activity involving legal products.